GOD
U.F.O.
ANTICHRIST

GOD
U.F.O.
ANTICHRIST

MICHAEL D. HAMILTON

ARPress
ILLUMINATING IDEAS.
EMPOWERING VOICES

ARPress
45 Dan Road Suite 5
Canton MA 02021

Hotline: 1(888) 821-0229
Fax: 1(508) 545-7580

Ordering Information:

Quantity sales. Special discounts are available on quantity purchases by corporations, associations, and others. For details, contact the publisher at the address above.

Printed in the United States of America.

ISBN-13:   Softcover   979-8-89330-118-2
                eBook   979-8-89330-119-9

Library of Congress Control Number: 2024901294

CONTENTS

DEDICATION

My honor has to solely give it to God Himself. I do not consider myself as the most intelligent person or the most imaginative person by far. But through meditation he makes me more special he can make all of us special if you only believe in your heart he is real. When I am weak he makes me stronger. When I am sad he makes me happy. For no other can make that happen for me but only him that is my dedication because with Him, I am nothing truly. I was full of anger, full of hate. He turn it into laughter and joy praise and full dedication and kisses to the Almighty God.

ACKNOWLEDGMENT

Truth in worshipping and praise and the improvement in our universe has no limitations. To learn that he and only he worshipping God himself has the leader of our universe; and our true existence depends solely on him; is truly vital to obtain and understand. To obtain this teaching is going to an non-denominational church call Church of God and Christ. Who conveyed to me that worshipping God is a vehicle to going to past the heaven's ; in meditation into God's courts or alter. Once reaching that area leaving your Earthly body through this meditation; you can obtain knowledge and power through God benevolence. Learning that God is real and to receive this knowledge through God by learning from the Church of God and Christ; how praise is in fact a vehicle. In retrospect through Jesus Christ asking forgiveness of your sins and then praising God; we as humans beings in the flesh can get knowledge why we are here? Where are we going in the future? In the binary world or some call the matrix. It all started with the Church of God and Christ.

What I like to convey to everyone in the world, do not in this time put your faith in the world we live in but your faith in God. In writing this book, if you think anything is false or fake take up your cross; and except God in your heart and start a personal relationship with God; so your teaching directly comes from him; that is what I did as a human being in binary world. I made God talk to me if I call on his name he has to answer that is the law's of the universe. As long as I accepted his son in my heart first and ask forgiveness of my sins. Second, he has to respong; see God has law's also to abide by also. He gives us choice that's a law he has to give us. A God cannot make us worship him but when we call his name for help in all sincerity he has to come. So I was in trouble in my life about to commit murder and had much hate; in my heart through a loveless childhood and was going to make the world pay for their sins; through death. Only a God could have changed me I had several guns pulled on me before the age of ten; been in so many fights I cannot remember them all how terrible. To hurt people and I enjoyed it. To obtain goodness in your hearts and its not easy that why we must always try to seek him because without him death draw nigh in each of us only reason I am still alive to write this book is because of God truly. Amen

INTRODUCTION

In the beginning, when I first got into the church I never knew how you can become close to God. In this book, I am compelled to tell the story of how this was accomplished and achieved by believing that you can have a true relationship with Him. In my early life I never really cared about anything.

About the time I reached high school, I was in many bad fights and had a very bad reputation. I had been in so many fights that I couldn't even remember who I had an issue with.

I was also very unhappy with my life. My ambition was to be like my uncles and cousins who had also established bad relationships and we were actually known to be a family not to trust because they were responsible for many murders in the city. I used to practice boxing and fighting; wanting to be just like my family and to become a murderer, and rob banks like my uncles and cousins, but God had another plan for me.

Through Him, I cheated death and all my friends with whom I wanted to commit murders and who are no longer on Earth. It was nothing being an Afro-American in the hood to be killed or to kill, became it was the way of life. By the age of 16, I had several guns pulled on me and somehow through the Grace of God, I am here now.

Anyone who has lived in the hood and grew up in that environment can concur with what I am conveying. I remember vividly the first time a gun was pulled on me. I was with my friends and we were being chased. I slipped and fell and the guy had a gun to my head.

The evil inside of me yelled out.

I specifically said to him, "Pull the trigger or get off of me."

At the age of 15, I had no fear of dying; he saw no fear in my eyes but he got off of me, laughed, and walked away. He probably didn't know that if he would have pulled the trigger, I would have taken that death without blinking because I was so unhappy from the lack of love from my family.

I did not have much of a relationship with my father or mother or brother and sisters who only criticized me and I gave that negativity back to the streets in fights, not fearing death at all. I want to make note, I never grew up in the church, and never intended to know the Maker who created us all.

I was going to extend the Martin name which was very well-known in the city as fighters and killers. My intentions and ambitions were to kill and never stop. I was going to surpass my family, from my great uncles to my uncles and my existing cousins.

I remember going to prison to visit my uncles and cousins at an early age. One of my uncles was in Leavenworth Penitentiary and made a living with my cousins robbing banks. He was one of the individuals I looked up to follow in his footsteps in life.

At 13, me and my uncle, who was the same age as me, and his older brother who robbed banks were in Leavenworth. They had robbed a bank and left the money at my Grandmother's house so I and my uncle found the money and were playing in the bed, throwing it up in the air and having fun trying to count all.

The reason why I put this story in the book is that I truly had intentions of murder and deceitfulness in my mind constantly. I was a danger to myself and many others; one of my plans was to rob banks and start fires all over the city, including the police stations so I can get away with a lot of money through diversions.

At 16 I had all this planned out. Anyone, I mean, anyone who would have gotten in my way I would have been killed instantly. I remember getting into many fights constantly. I recall I had one fight, up the street from my house, where I slammed the guy's head on concrete; he later killed his girlfriend and stabbed her 24 times.

My mother told me, "Boy you are not going to live long if you keep this up."

At that time I had so many negative thoughts and things going on in my life I was not listening to anyone. However, one particular day, I was with a girl who was older than me. I wanted to sleep with her. I believe she knew this so she invited me to church with her... this particular Church was the church of God and Christ so I agreed.

The only reason I went along with her was that I was hoping that this was my opportunity to sleep with her but that didn't happen. Instead, I met something which was way more powerful than my base desires.

Light of all lights, a king of kings, a love of all loves.

I saw a light over me, blinding me, telling me to sift the darkness and cast the Shadow out of me. During that first hour in the Church of God in Christ, I saw demons being cast out of one lady who fell to the ground; it was like a war zone in this small Church.

Good and evil were at hand.

The lady fell back on the floor as if something invisible had touched her or hit her with a giant hammer. My heart was bleeding and it felt like my chest was caving in. The light which was overshadowing me was piercing my soul, my mind, and my very being.

The crazy thing was I didn't want to kill no more.

I didn't want to die no more.

I didn't want to sleep with many girls anymore.

All I wanted was to meet this deity who could change me, who was unchangeable. I have never in my life felt fear before until then; I never had a trembling bone in my body, because I didn't fear death until then.

I, for the first time, felt true fear in a small Church where I saw a light of all lights. So no one, and I mean, no one can tell me that there is not a God. I feel that if I would never have been brought into that church that day, it would have been my mission in life to destroy a city and kill many; pure hate was reigning over my heart.

I had no conscience, no love for others, and only sought glorification for myself with greed and selfishness. I can remember another incident when I was 13 years old. My uncle had a party at my aunt's house where I saw women walking half-naked. It was a cocaine party and they totally forgot they had two 13-year-old boys watching the entire thing.

This is the type of life I lived.

Even after being saved I still delivered marijuana throughout the city for my father with his friends to make money. This is the life I lived. I remember my senior year, my father knocking on the door asking for money to go and buy crack to support his habit.

While most kids were living a normal life preparing for college I was dealing with a father who talked about killing my mom every week after doing crack. The only reason why I am here today is by the grace of God above. In fact, He gave me sanity in the midst of the chaos that comes with having a dysfunctional household. To this day I don't know how I survived this.

I also know many kids in America have dealt with these problems or much worse than what I had to face. Also, believe me when I say I am leaving lots of stories out to shorten this introduction.

There are many crazy stories in the family I grew up in. But this is not the story that I want to convey. The story I want to convey in *Heavenly Thoughts* is the one of my Heavenly Father who raised me in those times. He is my father; the one I communicated with and I shall share what I learned with you in this book.

I intended to write this book many years ago but I felt the world wasn't ready in the 80s to understand what I'm about to convey. I always say God is a jealous God but in many ways, He's a lonely guy. Through religion and limitations from man's perspective, we cannot handle much in our brains if we knew the truth that has been hidden from us and I won't say any names. I believe in this day and time in the 2000's, we will learn how to handle these truths.

So that's why, I've been silent since the 80s, until now, watching others to see if they would come close to what God has shown me which is a beautiful thing.

Now I should finish this introduction to begin my story of God speaking to me in my room. He talked about many subjects with no boundaries which I could handle in my mind. Some things I would not ask because my mind could not handle the truth.

So let's begin.

I hope you all read this book and keep a clear mind in the hope of becoming closer to God who I love and cherish. I do this not for the glorification of myself but so all can have agape love with the Father on Earth and in Heaven forever more.

I

GIFTS

To start off, let's begin with the gifts we have been granted by God in this world. Everything on Earth is a replica of what's in heaven. On Earth, you have eyes to see, ears to hear, a mouth to eat, and a nose to smell but does that make you a complete human for this world?

The answer might not be as easy as you think it to be. On the outlook, it may seem to be enough but to make yourself complete as a human being you must have a relationship of trust, faith, and belief in God.

With the belief that when you talk to Him, you will be able to do so with your spiritual eyes that will help you see his majesty, the spiritual mouth to savor his blessings, ears, and nose to smell and hear of his wonders. All your five senses will drive you closer to Him and strengthen the relationship you build with God.

The million-dollar question should be, how do you get those five gifts?

The first pre-requisite to getting honored with those five gifts is that you must believe in and worship God. As you do so, remember that you must go into his court with praise.

You can think of praise as a vehicle traveling from Earth to Heaven. Think of it as a means to transport you into paradise to witness God's presence.

When you get into his chambers after praising and glorifying Him as a means of worship, your next step has to be to talk to God and develop a spiritual relationship with the Heavenly father.

After that you may ask, what do I get in return for worshipping and praising Him?

When you start building a relationship with God, you will, in turn, begin to receive gifts from God. You will be able to hear Him and receive His messages to heal the sick, to see the future, to speak in languages you never knew, and above all, it will help you ward off evil from those you love.

Praise is a powerful tool. You can correlate it with the food that you can give God in return for His love and favors. Again, it's not something God can force you into. God can not force you to praise or worship Him. It is indeed your choice. A choice that you consciously have to make so you can come closer to God. You have to listen to the voices within; whispers that originate from your soul, yearning for God's remembrance.

The more you praise Him, the deeper you go into his chambers and the more you talk to Him, you will not just become valuable in His eyes, but you will also notice that people around you will start to value and honor you more than they ever did. In turn, you become a valuable soul on Earth.

But how does that happen? How do you suddenly become so precious to the world?

God blesses you with the power to do the same things that Jesus did on Earth. God wants us to have a relationship with Him, not just in Heaven but also in this life, on Earth.

He has destined for us the same gifts and powers that He bestowed Jesus with. But for that, we have to walk on the same path. He wants us to get there and have them. But to get there is totally up to us. It is our responsibility, our sole journey.

But then we all think at times that every time we get a bit closer to God, we tend to mess up and end up falling from grace. This is also true for me. There are times when even I think this way.

But is it really God's truth?

Yes, we make mistakes, and we mess up and fall but that doesn't mean God leaves us. It just means that we missed the mark to become mutants for God. The relationship still stands true, the love is still there. So what don't we have? Just the power to read minds and heal the sick etc.

" 5 Let your conduct be without covetousness; be content with such things as you have. For He Himself has said, "I will never leave you nor forsake you."

-Hebrews 13:5

Let's go back to treating praise as the food you can give to God.

Do you ever look up at the sun from the earth and think of how it's the source of life here? We do that often, don't we? Similarly, look up at the heavens and you will know that God is the supreme source of life everywhere.

 When you praise him, the instruments and the songs you sing for Him are played in the heavens. That means, the more we praise Him in the heavens from the Earth, the more blessings and gifts he will send down to all of us in return.

If you want to walk on water, you can do that through praise and communication with Him. If you want to heal your mom from cancer, through praise and communication you can.

You want to protect your family from drugs or gun violence? I did that through praise and communication with God. Once my brother got robbed and was pushed to the ground. The men fired at him but the bullet luckily missed him. Today, he is still here with us, enjoying all of God's gifts.

Last year the same incident happened to his son, about twenty years later. Again, it was another miss fire with a machine gun and he was able to escape. These are the situation that reignites our faith in God. That's God and His gifts.

There is one fatal thing I forget to convey in all of this that is so important: asking for forgiveness of your sins or he will not answer. He will not answer to your praise or worship.

Initially, I used to ask Him what I needed and then asked forgiveness from Him for all the wrongs that I had done that day. . But here is what I observed when I switched it.

Once you make it a part of your routine to first praise Him, and it goes past the earth, the galaxies, the heavens, beyond the saints, and is sung in God's presence, you start to feel more powerful, at ease, and content.

It feels like whatever we say next will be heard with happiness in His court. Our praise will help us get the gifts from God.

You feel as though God is anointing you with his glory.

I have to tell you this story of when I was seventeen years old. One day when I was in my room, I was indeed in God's Court. My biological father opened the door to my room and the look on his face was shattering. I will never forget that moment as long as I am on Earth.

My father paused in shock, and I don't know what he saw., maybe God's anointed power? But his eyes became wider and he slammed the door and never returned. He never talked about it even until he died. My mother or family never mentioned it also. My siblings never knew too. They always thought I was a weird person at a weird place in my life but they didn't know that place saved me from dying on the streets like most of my friends.

Being in God's courts is such a beautiful place to be. When you open your eyes to return to Earth again after that long, spiritually intimate meditation, it's truly the best experience a human being can ever encounter. There's no beachy breeze, no mountain lush, and no ocean shimmer that you can compare with it.

There is eternal serenity, warmth, and de-stressing bliss there.

When in fact you open your eyes, you can tell that you left Earth and transcended to a heavenly place of anointment and now you have returned.

This is the beginning of the process through worship and praise entering his courts and transcending back down and just feeling His love. You are establishing a new relationship like a friendship. You don't meet a new friend and tell him about all your secrets initially.

For the relationship to become more trustworthy and fulfilling, the communication between you and your friend must be very strong. Similarly to have a fulfilling relationship with God, there is no other requirement but communication.

There is no difference between earth and heaven, It's an exact replica.

Never forget that, be it the negative or the positives that you face.

You would say negative in heaven? Yes truly.

Heaven has had its share of problems like Earth has its problems. I remember talking to God about gang violence and God told me we have dealt with the same here. But that is something I will talk about in detail later in the book.

First of all, I must get you to the point of receiving the gifts of spiritual senses. Remember to ask for forgiveness of your sins. Worship, and praise, let them enter His courts and get the gifts of speaking in heavenly languages. Don't forget that you've already asked Jesus Christ to enter your life and heart.

After that, you have to start taking the five steps that will help you go along this process and access the amazing powers that God has destined for you.

After 3 years of doing this, I began to get afraid because I started to read people's minds. I know, it sounds crazy but it's the truth.

One time I went to see a pastor preach and the whole time while he was preaching, I was in God's Court. I didn't even notice that he was paying full attention to me during the sermon. He came to me and started crying and dropped down to his knees when the sermon ended.

The mere fact of even thinking about it is crazy.

It happened to me on several occasions. I used to know people's names before they even told me. In life, you never get these gifts taken back from you. They just get tarnished in time if you do not use them.

But as long as you're in the physical state, you can always go back and have them re-polished. These gifts remain with you for a lifetime.

I could feel spirits in the house. I can feel when bad things are about to happen around me. The power of these gifts is truly incredible. These gifts are available to all mankind. Whenever you choose to gain a spiritual mind and body and soul, you will find them waiting on your path to God.

II

THE BIBLE

Before I get started, I must say some are going to be upset. However, you must remember that the Bible is divine and it is the word of God. God has indeed given us a great tool to learn from as a book of instructions and guidelines and provides us daily motivation in the form of the Bible.

As bitter as it may sound, it has been chopped up like a cow at the slaughterhouse. The word of God has been put back into the tombs claiming that it is only for the benefit of man.

There is a place in Dallas where they have a collection of all the different versions of the Bible as they kept being reworked and rewritten. In the last thirty years, I have been a witness to it myself. As a regular reader of the Divine book, I can spot the differences myself. In the meanings, the contexts, and the feel of the book.

It is no more the Bible, today. It's man-made. Men trying to intervene in God's decree and ruling. Everyone around the globe preaches from the Bible, saying it's the word of God.

But has the Bible remained Holy, and is it actually God's word?

That which is holy should not be touched to conform to each new generation. And no, we have got to stop telling the world that we're only trying to make its concepts easier for the younger generations to understand, trying to reduce its complexity and make it simpler with every revised version of its. Stop saying that because it doesn't add on. The sole reason behind this is the fact that our interventions and revisions of the original book of God only shrink the sanctitude of this scripture.

The church has hidden books over the years. But more importantly, the church has hidden knowledge over the years. This implies that the church has essentially hidden God's holy word over the years.

God's holy word has been chopped up, watered down, to the confinements of mankind's liking. We may please the generations as we evolve but we must be wary of the fact that God is well aware of it. Jesus knows it and so does the Holy Spirit. We're not fooling anyone but ourselves.

When I first read Genesis I was angry and confused. I wondered why my spirit felt perplexed. Why didn't I feel that spiritual connection as though God was directly addressing me through his scripture?

Why wasn't there the connection I should have felt?

It was very despairing, to be honest. I even questioned my spectrum of what I was doing wrong.

Then again, when I raised questions and said something about it, they said, "One day God will give you the wisdom to understand."

But what Godly wisdom can I attain from a man?

It's a chopped-up mess. When I started off this chapter, saying that I may upset and enrage a few of you, this is what I meant by it.

I knew that some of you may get mad and upset with me but I had to write it all down. I wanted to do my bit even if it did not please anyone for my actions are only to please God, and they must be, in all my aspirations.

I talked to a friend who's from the Middle East and he bragged about saying, "Our Quran has not been tampered with like you all Bible."

To be honest, I was left speechless. You might question why I didn't present a counter-argument. Well, I have been a witness to how it changes, in turn bringing about a contextual change in the divine book too. So, how could I?

I could not have argued with him. Martin Luther himself took seven books out of the Bible. People may present with a lot of arguments saying he revolutionized the generations that came next but it's baseless. In reality, it was only done because he wanted the Bible, God's own words to conform to his man-made theology.

Some religions accept certain books yet others don't accept the teachings of certain books because of their own beliefs. You really need God to be there to understand many of the Bible's interpretations. It is solely attributed to the fact that mankind has been tampering with the word of God for ages.

As I shed light on the concerning matter, it is also essential that we still uphold Bible's virtues and respect its sanctity. Bible is, indeed still divine in its purpose to change mankind and bring him closer to God. It is still a tool to help bring God closer in our lives. Yet, at the same time, it is of utmost importance to highlight to the world to not take the word of God away from us.

Please!

Quit messing with it.

Sometimes I think about how people leisurely express that they're atheists and no one is bothered or agitated about it. It's funny that when the same people meet someone pointing out flaws in how the context of God's word through the Bible has been changing throughout the centuries, they're upset, enraged, and tetchy about it.

How ironic is that?

I know that the church is going to get mad when I say this but for the sake of God, it is important to point the flaws out regardless criticism I may have to face for this. In the church, it's as if the Bible has become the king and God has become second.

In retrospect when we think about these matters, that's probably why the world and scientists have always been ahead of the church in doing the right thing and the church has always been second.

Once we put God first, and the Bible second as a tool, we will begin to see the world as we should. We'll be the first in this world, the leaders of the world.

At times I feel that the church is giving up and saying that these are the last days, and we're waiting for the rapture to come to see you later.

However, the church should man up and show God that she is worthy of saving this world with Jesus. Through God's help and teachings we can bring heaven to Earth.

The Bible is once again a divine book of God, but it is not God. It is only a tool to bring you closer to God. Nothing more; nothing less.

But for all of us to get the quintessence of the holy scripture, let all the books come out and be read. Let the full Bible be accessible to men around the globe so it can be read, understood, and implied in its entirety while keeping its actual concepts and theology intact.

Let all the scrolls come out even if they may not please the entire society. We are ready.

The Vatican let all be read. We are ready and grown-ups. We have enough to know the truth. We are entering the age of Aquarius. Let that be known, let there be read. Let us decide what word is God's word and what is divine for our hearts. Because if we love God we will be able to decipher what is good for our soul and what will help us grow closer to God. Amen.

When the great flood happened, it was God's way of slowing man's progress in learning. Angels took it into their own hands to speed up man's process of learning. But that wasn't their job. It was God's job. Aliens or other humanoids from other places were put in check who threaten the pace of mankind's learning speed. So they both had to be excluded from the equation because they affect man's growth.

Man was not ready for flight yet but in places like India, Egypt, and its vicinity, there was flight. The developments and introduction of Lazar technology, batteries, and levitation enhanced the minds of giant boulders. Giants had their cities and aliens had theirs. All in conglomerate with mankind but we were not ready with such technologies.

There were laboratories that were researching men and animals, mixing and matching them up. God looked upon the Earth and saw the things that had taken over his creation for their own lust and slavery. We were used for their own convenience.

The flood came and was used for washing out and purifying Earth for the sake of mankind. It was a cleansing to show who's the Lord of lords and the God of Gods.

The rain came down endlessly. Atlantis was flooded all over and sunk to the bottom of the ocean due to the torrents. This was not just a cleansing of Earth, it was also Heaven in the Book of Enoch.

It was more than rain. It was gaining control of what God created for men. Mankind's clock was sped up thousands of years and God could not have that.

Now, we're about to face that time again. The seven seals are releasing and the skies are filled with cloaking crafts. There are going to be rough times ahead and these are all the indications pointing toward it.

From the caverns, strange creatures like Giants are going to emerge and even stranger things will walk out of the sea.

They say history repeats itself and it can't be more true than this reality. I am now giving a fair warning when our government starts releasing the truth about things like pyramids on Mars, the Stargates on Earth, and Atlantis rising again from the sea.

Don't freak out and abolish God.

Don't burn your Bibles.

History is repeating itself.

But the new generation needs more knowledge and that is because the Bible, in its form today, is not enough to sustain. We must prepare ourselves because it's coming sooner than later.

All the books need to be released to prove God's existence and glory. He came and saved us in that flood once, then later saved us again with his son.

So why are we, Mankind, His creations, holding out on valuable knowledge in His holy scripture?

There are those out there preaching to the world that we come from Mars and that Mars was destroyed. Then we moved here and started a colony.

Some are preaching that we come from a matrix system created by an alien race of celestial beings.

So, why are we holding back God's own words? Why are we concealing the truth and letting people go astray easily?

We must take stronger measures and quick actions now, or we will be fighting a losing battle. God exists, and the Bible is his tool. But his tool has been reshaped over the years.

This new generation needs more to sustain itself. Their curious minds must find the right answers, which will only be possible when they decipher the complete truth.

I call this age the Google age of deceit. Our action is mandatory. Let us not have God keep saving us all the time. We must save ourselves with his tools like the Bible and his knowledge.

May we all find the courage and strength to do it.

Amen.

III

CREATION OF MAN

There are a lot of theories surrounding the creation of man.

How long has man been in existence?

The conversation is argumentative.

I believe the oldest human skull found is 4.2 million years old. How remarkable is that.

Can the seed of Adam match up to a 4.2 million old skull?

Does Genesis in the Bible, with Christians and all their theories of God, their Creator, stand up to make a valid argument?

Are they right about the Big Bang theory?

Are they right that we were once apes or descendants of apes?

Where is your faith now?

As scientists, we have proof that creation is a myth.

Any atheist can say where is your God now?

One can say that your Bible only goes back 10,000 years in history. Your place where the hands of the Almighty God conceived Adam and Eve is null and void. We have full ownership and many skulls that go back millions of years that you can touch and feel like our famous Lucy. Creation by the hands of God with Adam and Eve is nothing but a story in folklore that's been passed down through history as bedtime stories like us believing in Santa Claus.

How do we argue, then?

Evolution is an undeniable fact. It is a part of every living thing. One is black, one is white, one is red, and another is yellow, and similarly, all the rainbow colors. That's the evolution of man through various temperatures around Earth. Over the years, there has been an evolution of the human skull.

The smarter we get, the smaller our skulls get.

It is reversed, where I believe it should get bigger.

Unfortunately, that is not the case with men. Adam and Eve, Cain and Abel; the story goes that their children and so on all come to form what we have today.

Now I have a problem with that.

For one, if that's possible, we would be all products of incest. So, in asking God to clarify this incest problem and the problem of us coming from apes, the answer was another group of people before Adam and Eve.

Before the Garden of Eden, a race of people roamed the Earth with the dinosaurs for many years. They were the Neanderthals. They were different than men today. Over millions of years, there was a form of evolution all through those years. But Adam, Eve, Cain, Abel, and the other children were lost in this transition by going against God, and the Neanderthals gained by becoming more intelligent.

They spread their seed of intelligence by eating an apple that God did not want them to eat. This transformation of these tribes now can possess the mistakes and sins of Eve. The Earth with Mankind boosts from God to populated, educated, and intuitiveness. Mankind did not come from apes or monkeys because if we did occur through evolution, the animals wouldn't be here today. They would have been a part of us.

If that had been the case, if Adam, Eve, Cain, and Abel had mated with the monkeys or apes and it worked, you would have one smaller version of Bigfoot.

Just joking.

I must also convey that the Garden of Eden was not that big of a place. That is why we, as men, have never found it.

Besides, if we did find it probably would not be a good thing because the tree of Life exists. God's angels have the tree of Life heavily guarded. I know scientists have proof of this skull called Lucy.

But you can try and match man's DNA with monkeys or apes, and it will not work. I can say that I have Neanderthal in me, but I cannot say that I have apes or monkeys in me. For the sake of humanity and Neanderthals, I have never seen to this day a monkey or ape going to a cave and drawing horses and cows, and that will never happen anyway.

However, like monkeys and apes in the trees, we are genetically inclined to have a roof or caverns. We are not strong enough to climb trees the way they do because we lack that physical strength and structure. Their feet are more balanced than ours.

Unlike them, we hunt and eat meat as omnivores, which is a huge difference. Evolution usually doesn't change your eating habits; to search for fruits and remain herbivores for thousands of years, you don't suddenly switch to meat.

Now back to the garden of Eden; after Cain killed Abel, he wandered off and found something that was truly similar to him. And that which was similar to him wasn't as polished, wasn't that smart, but it did have sex appeal, and he mated with a Neanderthal woman. Through that seed of the Apple, instantly, the babies were intelligent. The brains and skulls were smaller.

That is why in the Bible, it seemed like it was Adam, Eve, Cain, and Abel, and then suddenly, we jumped up, and a couple of scriptures later, we have cities. Way too direct and vague.

To be honest, this is one subject that really bothers me as a Christian.

Did we just come from Adam, Eve, Cain, and Abel?

Through the form of incest?

If that's the case, we all know that incest can cause physical deformities, psychological problems, and various diseases.

There were two versions of humanity. We mate, and that is what we have today. There is no difference between tribes and races mating today; we all have different things to offer. Some races might have different technical advantages that others might want to obtain.

Now, back to incest. I once was sold an inbred dog. The dog was so crazy my relatives were scared to come by. When I tried to breed the dog, all four litters died except two. Nature would not let her have pups. She was the most vicious of all my dogs because of the inbreeding.

To bring up this point, if the children of Adam and Eve had just bred with each other, there would only be crazy people all around. Nature would not allow it. Cain had children; matter of fact, my favorite of his offspring is Enoch. The book of Enoch is great.

Nevertheless, man and Neanderthal came together to form a perfect match. Man, after eating that apple became intuitive. The Neanderthals were not knowledge seekers. They were complacent human beings who were not very intuitive. The eating of that apple was the beginning of man and his intuitiveness. The Neanderthal man is similar to the native tribes in our jungles today; very complacent and traditional.

If we are to go to Africa and meet the pygmies, we'll have a better understanding of the whole situation. They have no exposure, so it doesn't mean they lack intelligence, only intuitiveness. There won't be a plane flying out of the jungle soon. But they have intelligence that helps them survive the jungle better than all of us. That's why Cain bred with the natives of the land. We and our cities have more of that piece of apple that was bitten in the Garden of Eden.

If I took a woman from the pygmy people, bore a child with her, and then raised that child in the city, the child would be just as intelligent as any other child. That is a very fast transition from one generation to making a difference, from parents growing up in a remote tribe to their child growing up to be a doctor.

That is the power of God's apple in the Garden of Eden. To change how humanity thinks; about building cities through masonry. That is why in Genesis, literally in a blink of an eye after consuming that apple, we had cities and tall buildings. The bite of that apple triggered intuition, which now exists in us to seek greater knowledge.

Evolution would have been a lot slower if that apple hadn't been eaten. That small act sped up evolution from simple mammals like the natives we see today to us, humans. But it also brought along cars, planes, trucks, and cities as we evolved. We didn't need God anymore because we became small mini Gods with our agenda, thoughts, and plans.

God was indeed angry because we no longer had respect for our Creator.

How dare Cain be smart to God after murdering Abel!

Cain sarcastically answered to God, "Am I my brother's keeper?"

That wouldn't have happened before that apple was eaten. We walk around naked like the natives of today, and the women still walk around with no bra on. Natives around the world have similar worldly traditions. They sit around campfires and dance to their music and language.

In a way, I think that is beautiful. Instead of fast life and perplexity, they lead a simple life.

I believe God would eventually let us eat that apple, but it would have been the right time and place after him teaching us.

IV

THE PARALLEL UNIVERSE

I call this the parallel universe but my son said I cannot call this that but, oh well. I think it's a good name because we cannot see them. I must begin to talk about the parallel universe which is a realm where everything is happening around us and we cannot see.

There's so much activity around us, and so many spirits surrounding us daily that it is safe to say that each of us is never truly alone, even when we're in private. Those who think they have secrets, or assume that they have things hidden in the closet must realize that nothing is ever truly hidden in the world we live in. It is only temporarily concealed from sight.

The Earth is teeming with life and also teeming with many spirits. There's an argument that states that spirits and ghosts are one and the same. To me that is irrelevant. The focal point is that even in a parallel universe they exist.

In the Bible, it first said the Holy Ghost, and now it says the Holy Spirit. Is it a ghost or a spirit?

It's irrelevant; just know that it is there.

Let's talk about this dilemma of the Holy Ghost or the Holy Spirit.

I called him the exhortation spirit. He roams the Earth to give us an exhortation so we will not lose a life for that day. Once you begin to tap into the spiritual world, you might hear a voice warning you not to drive your car today or you hear a voice that tells you not to go out drinking with your friends that's the Holy Ghost talking to you.

It doesn't matter if you're Christian; it is there to save us all. It can be known through other names such as your conscience, spirit guides, etc. If it wasn't for the Holy Ghost, I would have died many years ago.

I was once at a stoplight at 3 in the morning, getting off from work. The light had just turned green and instead of moving forward, I just sat there not putting my foot on the gas.

A voice kept telling me, "Don't go, don't go."

If I hadn't listened and overruled the exhortation I would have been disintegrated by the CRX that came bulldozing through the light going over a hundred miles per hour. Now, mind you, the light had been green for a while. To others, I might have looked like an idiot, sitting at a green light but I've been through so many situations where he has saved me that I know his voice now.

Whenever you hear something telling you don't go that way don't overrule that.

Last summer, my stepdaughter was killed; she was shot nine times. The day before she was killed, I received many warning signs that something was going to happen to her. You see all our spirits are connected to each other and we know each other, if that makes sense.

Unfortunately, she was not listening to the warning signs that the Holy Ghost was giving to her. But we were connected in our spirits through love, so the Holy Ghost was giving me warning signs to try to save her.

I recall I was sitting outside the house of my ex at midnight and contemplating and going to talk to her because I knew something was going to happen very soon. I wrestled in my mind and my spirit to go into the house to talk to her. I had my 19-year-old son with me in the car and he'd just got off from work.

"Do you think it's okay to go in and talk to my stepdaughter before something drastic happens?" I asked him.

Then I looked up, and I saw her mother, my ex, walking around and I said, "I won't disturb the house today, I'll do it tomorrow for sure."

With that, we drove away. It turned out that tomorrow was too late, she was killed at 3 p.m. I had overruled the exhortation that was given to me to act at that time and the consequences were dire.

The Holy Ghost conveys its message quickly, at the right time, and at the right moment - if you do not listen, most of the time the consequences are fatal. It will not block you or hold you down, it speaks and gives exhortation more than once.

"Hear me when I speak," is the message that resonates loud and clear because usually if you don't listen is fatal. I have several stories to tell about the intervention of the Holy Spirit.

When I was in my twenties, I was working at the Marriott and there was a girl who liked me. This girl became very upset by the fact that I did not like her back. So one day she came in and started to argue with me, right outside, before we'd even stepped foot inside.

I found the argument to be pointless so I started to walk away. Something told me to turn and face her, and as I did, I couldn't believe what I was seeing. She was charging at me with a brick in her hand which was usually used as a door stop and then, she threw it at my head.

I'm sure that she could have done a lot of damage if I hadn't turned around. But this is not the end of the story. Even though the confrontation had started because she liked me, we were both fired on the spot and sent home right away.

Before she left she looked at me and said, "This is not the end of this."

That particular week my car had broken down, so I couldn't go home on my own after being fired from my job. I called my mother to come to pick me up. While waiting outside the Marriott, I kept hearing warning signs get up and leave now.

The Holy Spirit told me if I didn't leave now the consequences would be fatal. Now, mind you while I was waiting on my mother, there was no way for me to contact her. There were no cell phones at the time so

I couldn't tell her not to come to get me anymore. But I couldn't ignore the urgency in that voice.

I got up and walked down the street, got on the bus, and went home. Years later after moving to Atlanta, I moved back home to Kansas City. One day, I ran into a guy I vaguely remembered. He saw me and his eyes got big.

"Hey man, you're that dude who I've been waiting to talk to for so many years!" he said. "Do you remember me? I used to work security at the Marriott."

"Yes, I remember now," I told him.

"Man, seconds after you left the Marriott to walk down the street to the bus stop, a guy got out of the car with a 357 Magnum looking for you. He was out for blood and ready to take your life."

I was speechless but that's the power of the Holy Ghost.

When I look back, I couldn't see a reason for me to just get up and leave. It was a bright sunny day and my mother was coming to pick me up. But if I would have ignored the Holy Spirit I would have died that day.

I have so many stories I can tell you from car wrecks to close encounters of me getting shot where the Holy Spirit intervened and saved me.

My nephew asked me recently, "Uncle Vic, why do you ride around with the radio off in your car?"

The reason why is I cannot hear the Holy Spirit while driving. If everyone in their cars would put their cell phones down, and turn the music down I believe that we would have fewer fatalities on the road because the Holy Spirit will warn us when we are in danger.

I've had deers cover the front, I've had cars pull in front of me, and escaped death many times on the road through the Holy Spirit watching over me. You don't have to be a holy person for him to give you an exhortation, that's why it's called the Holy Ghost.

Now to further go into the parallel world some other spirits or ghosts are not so nice. Jealousy is a spirit, that also roams the Earth. There's also another Spirit that's called Greed. Another one that constantly perpetuates inside of us is power.

I will not give these spirits praise as they have started wars. They have hurt many and they exist in a parallel universe. The main reason why man took so long to become more intelligent in the universe is because of the warfare that exists on Earth's parallel universe. It's getting juicy now, right? Not to give man an excuse for his actions, but if a parallel war is going on it causes war in the physical realm too.

We know what's good for us but these spirits disrupt our growth as humans on Earth. Humans would have been much further along than others in the universe that God created. Others in the universe are not hindered like we are by ghosts or spirits.

I know some of you think the definition of a ghost is something that once lived in the physical realm. The definition of a spirit is something that never actually lived. Spirits can enter and disrupt those who are living in the physical realm. Actually, there's a fine line between ghosts and spirits - all I know is they're all there.

I have to also talk about the small little spirits that feel like bugs clamped on your back.

My daughter once got into a fight. She has anger issues and sometimes, she can become so infuriated that she can blank out and not remember what happened.

There are small spirits that can clamp on all of our bodies. Younger and weaker people are more susceptible like my daughter and others. They are anger creatures that increase your anger through the roof. When in this rampaging state, you will kill anything in your way.

I love it when people say let's focus on the positive because the positive is a form of spirit that is good. It wards off these creatures of anger. The amazing thing is that I know this yet I still let anger latch on my back. As humans when we feel anger, sometimes it is good and other times, it's not because others used us, lied to us, and stole from us.

It hurts to wonder about things like, "Why did she cheat on me? I was a great husband. Why did he kill thirty women?"

The answer is we are in the middle of spiritual warfare on Earth.

How do you combat such a force?

Seeking good spirits in the metaphysical like one talking to God is your best start. I had a person I met once who didn't believe in God, didn't believe in spirits and we were just a part of a matrix like the movies.

I say to you, non-believers of spirits, be careful when you do this. It's going to be like using a Ouija board. You open portals for evil spirits in your house and the only way to get them out is going to God. That's the only way I could make you believe because evil spirits reside on Earth through the sins of Adam and Eve and react faster to us.

You might say what do you mean?

Man's ears have been clouded from hearing good spirits including the voice of God. This is spiritual warfare that was started in the garden of Eden when Eve first disregarded God's command. Now we have spirits of jealousy and rage anger that power and greed roaming the Earth to hinder man's relationship with God and the heavens above.

Christians believe that heaven will one day become physical and be on Earth - that's impossible. Heaven on Earth means that when Jesus the Messiah comes back he will end this warfare that preceded the 4 days of Adam and Eve. That's what's meant by the saying heaven is now on Earth. Man will be free from this constant temptation of evil spirits, he will seek God's way and also become more powerful and spiritually mined through God's help.

You will not have to do what I do now, which is to avoid listening to the radio to make sure God's voice is talking to me from the parallel universe. You will hear only God's voice and you will know when He speaks to you. You will not be tempted by these evil little creatures that latch on your back and dull your sense, making you forget the atrocities you just committed.

The rich won't keep getting richer, idolizing money that is ill-begotten through greed. Sex offenders who are obsessed with pornography will no longer exist through the grace of God. The evil spirits among us will be put in check.

Before I end this chapter on the parallel universe I'll tell one ghost story. Sometimes ghosts get trapped between two worlds, I do not know why.

I was working at the casino in the late 90s at the bar on Halloween.

"Does anyone have any scary stories about ghosts?"

This one African-American lady got very upset and fixed me with a mean stare.

The bar started hooting. It was obvious she had a story to tell. Luckily, she didn't need a lot of encouragement. So she began to tell her story.

She had a house she had paid for in the Intercity. Her husband who came to the casino with her was ex-Vietnam and feared nothing nor was scared of him. He worked as a bouncer in another bar close to my house.

She said she only found out after buying the house that four people had been killed in the house. Apparently, it was a drug deal gone bad. You'd think these spirits were ghosts who would have left Earth but that's not the case.

She said every time they tried to rent the house the people experienced so much paranormal activity that they would always try to break the lease.

After a while, it got so bad that the house was torn down to relinquish the problem of evil experiences. Spirits just still roam the Earth I don't know why but it is what it is. A parallel universe is as active as the physical you can only imagine just as many people we have on Earth, and we have just as many spirits or ghosts, that's amazing, right?

So if you're feeling very angry now you know why?

If you're feeling to cheat on your wife now you know why?

If you're idolizing money in which money has become a God on Earth now you know why?

If you idolize a car, do now you know why?

These habits that we have, drugs, sex, power, manipulation, lies, deceit, and even suicide are all spiritual parasites in our world our physical world.

That's why the Holy Spirit is so important for life on Earth. It is a spirit of exhortation that extends your time so you may one day talk to God. Even right now, he is telling someone, "Don't drive your car today," "Don't go in the woods today," "Don't fly your plane today," "Go to the basement, a tornado is coming."

The Holy Spirit does that for all of us and Mankind. No other spirit does that but the Holy Spirit or the Holy Ghost.

So now you must believe in ghosts because the Holy Ghost is looking out for you.

V

THE SAVIOR JESUS CHRIST

I really don't know where to start totally with Jesus.

Let's start when I ask Jesus to come down to my room to talk to me. Because Jesus changes the game. You know we have the right to summon his Spirit, how beautiful, right?

It's funny; I laugh when spirits come into your room they usually stand in the corner of the room. Maybe it's because we are not so clean on Earth. Nevertheless, His spirit is so warm, soft, and gentle. I don't even think I can put it in words.

Imagine if possible, the nicest person you ever met on Earth, multiplied by a thousandth power; that's Jesus coming into your room. To touch his soft spiritual hand is amazing. That very same hand has a hole in it.

To hear his voice is like hearing the voices of a thousand angels and all that. Jesus Christ is a really, really beautiful soul and Spirit I cannot say this enough with my earthly body to fulfill this justification. He changed the way heaven looks at us, he changed the way God looks at us. He made us worthy again or we would have all been obliterated like Sodom and Gomorrah.

He gave us value when we should not have any value. Also, he's very understanding and knows what temptation is, he knows the war zone that we face down here. He knows our secrets our faults, our desires, and every inch of us.

Blessed be thy name, my savior whom I love; give me strength, kiss me on the cheek.

Isn't that awesome?

I can ask Jesus to come down and kiss me on the cheek and he will in spirit. We can go up to heaven in his courts and praise God. It's funny people are trying to get to heaven through worship but they don't know they can go to heaven every day.

Jesus did that.

If you want to walk on water, just talk to him.

If you want to hear the sick, just talk to him.

If you want to get over drugs, just talk to him.

You can summon him in your room whenever you feel like it; his dying on the cross gave us that ultimate power.

I recently came close to killing someone because my daughter was murdered. Through faith, I asked him to come into my room to help me to talk about it; how awesome. See I'm a ratchet man still capable of murder. Once again Jesus stopped me from murdering another.

From the early part of my life even to now, through the power of Jesus, let no one, I mean, no one, say that Jesus didn't talk to you. They don't have that right. No one has the right to say who's going to heaven and who's going to hell. Only God and Jesus have that right. In this book, I don't seek glory; only glory to my God and Jesus and the Holy Spirit. I am just a messenger and no one can say otherwise.

Jesus gave us the power to go to heaven on a daily basis. Jesus gave us the power to ask for forgiveness of our sins to get closer to God. Jesus gave us the power to summon their holy spirits into our room; how powerful. The whole purpose of Jesus Christ coming down is that we can talk to God.

I have a relationship with God and him. I take a shower first by asking for forgiveness of my sins, then as a vehicle through worship and praise, I enter God's Heaven. When you open your eyes again you're back on Earth; Jesus did that.

Now I must go to the negative side of Jesus. The one thing that upset him is when we make the father upset. We have done this many times. I heard the pastor say that God never changes; that Jesus never changes. Through the stupidity of souls, we all have evolved. I guess that's a nice way to put it.

Jesus changed heaven and Earth; through him, all have evolved - all have changed. That's why I can kiss Christ's hands and kiss his soft feet and bow down. Through my selfishness, I don't do that too many times. Like we say that in the hood that's real talk.

I don't understand how people on Earth are still waiting for the Messiah. No prophet can change heaven and Earth but Jesus. I asked God, "Why do they consider him a prophet?"

The answer I got back was one of the main reasons in the Bible. There were some issues with the apostles and Mary Magdalene's relationship with Jesus. Maybe I shouldn't bring this up because of all the glorious things he's done for heaven and Earth. But apparently, in history, this must be brought up to vex my soul.

You see Jesus loved everyone. The past of your sins doesn't separate you from him; how beautiful.

Mary loved Jesus and he loved her and apparently, the church tried to stifle that relationship. It is also one of the reasons why Judas deceived Jesus and why he is considered just a prophet. Let's say for the sake of argument Jesus married Mary Magdalene. They bore a child before he was crucified.

I don't have a problem with that but the church does. It doesn't change who he was what he was for and his love for the almighty God heaven and us. We should even be included in that list. If you look at Jesus, our sins didn't affect him from looking at the true us.

And that's not much to look at.

Statements like, "Forgive them, Father. They know not what they do."

All your sins; that's evolving - that's power. No, no one can dare touch the subject of sin with God but Jesus. No prophet in history has the power to do so. I don't care if Jesus kissed Mary on the lips a thousand times; he changed heaven, Earth, and the universe.

VI

AMERICA - THE CHOSEN ONE

The land of milk and honey, a land in which God has always had his hand involved. Yet there is another hand involved in America. There's always been this seed that lingers in the corridors, that divides us; in which hatred breeds like a mold in the basement that is waiting to claim its victim.

While God has chosen us as a nation that can provide for and help others in need, which has such a great land mass to feed the world, this mold is still in the shadows, waiting to consume us and destroy us from the inside.

When writing our constitution, God was in the room but so was that seed of hatred and greed. Amid all this chaos, somehow, God's words were put in place to help America grow. In that room where the Constitution was made where all men were created equal, in God, we trust.

What a beautiful concept to build a nation to become one with God, not through religion, but through purpose and honesty to make a nation better and the world better to lead by example of our Constitution by God being in that room. As always, unfortunately, where there's light there's always darkness and in that darkness, there's always deception.

The Constitution with its freedom, with God's words in their hands, we have hatred trying to divide and jeopardize this land of milk and honey. The land of milk and honey and our Constitution go together to help people and the world come together as one nation under God or one world under God. To not be a superpower to take and destroy and control but a big brother to show all are created equal around the world.

But that mode keeps surfacing inside of America a mode that divides us and takes away our Christianity. What separates us from light and that black mode can destroy us within; with greed and segregation, our enemies overcome us. I pray that God will help us through these trying times.

The day that we seek equality among ourselves, not greed, hatred, or degradation. God could easily give this land of milk and honey to someone else to leave the charge of responsibility to feed the world without greed but with love and Christianity.

So we have a choice to love each other to help each other and help others. It is up to us to destroy that inner mode between black and white. Where all are created equal to help us and the world. If the people are hungry let them come, if the people are being abused, let them come. If the people are trying to make a better family for their kids let them come.

That's why God gave this land.

Not to divide us but to help us with what we have done, that's why we are a blessed nation. Once upon a time, slaves went to Canada and Mexico because they were hungry and afraid; now we let others come here because they're hungry and afraid.

We must learn from history and never go back.

All great nations have started off on the backs of slaves; you must get past that point, ask for forgiveness and use that energy to help others with God's grace, power and harmony through Christianity and prayer.

Of course, everything is done in moderation and we can't let our borders be over run but let's not forget what we are here for. A melting pot for the world that all people can come here and seek a better life.

Also, the ones are already here should be able to keep there freedom through God's grace.

Let's not dismantle our constitution.

Yes, there were some things that had to be changed dealing with segregation but now they are changed, let's move forward in harmony, peace, and prayer.

VII

ALIENS AND UFOs

N ow let's get into the topic that's sweeping America: UFOs. The Bible doesn't talk about dinosaurs but we know they existed. The Bible also doesn't talk about UFOs but we're finding out that they do exist. Both of these things have existed in our lives for as long as humans have existed as depicted in cave paintings and other relics.

You might say that the Bible doesn't bring this subject up at all. But, that's not the purpose of the Bible; it is only there to give the history of man and his relationship with God and how to maintain it, not to discuss what He created before and after us. As a matter of fact, God is still creating things right now, as you are reading this.

He did not stop with man, I am sorry to tell you that. Mankind has no control over what God created.

Didn't Lucifer get mad when God created man?

God the Creator, never stops creating, just like He never stops loving the things He created. Scientists said the universe is getting bigger and there seeing fewer stars every year; that's God's doing. Let's get into pre-flood before God rained down on the Earth you think we were alone? No.

It was one big party down here. Atlantis had got flying ships flying around with exotic buildings and UFOs were messing with man's DNA to satisfy themselves, to enslave us, and to be worshipped by them.

If you talk to natives all around the world then you will find out that they talked about the star people. They have vowed to return one day to reunite with us but in Atlantis, their plans for us were shattered. Their future for us was altered by the All-Mighty God. He showed his power like he did to Sodom and Gomorrah. He showed his face in the flood.

How dare you interfere with what I have created and modify what I have created? I am the God of Gods. I am the Creator of Creators; I am the ruler of the heavens. He took his hand and with water and tornadoes and lightning and heavy winds and smote them into the bottom abyss in the ocean. It was a city that will never be found again no matter how hard we look because they didn't leave, they faced the wrath of God alone.

Now on Earth, another party was going on about having sex with celestial beings. It is said that all the wire instruments, weird music, and strange drinks like beer were around because of them. To this day, we don't know who created beer. I think it came from the fallen angels. They also taught us how to make wine and appreciate marriage.

People sacrificed in the name of other Gods and Lords. Angels posing as Gods claimed to rule the Earth forever. The Giants had their own land and imposed their might on mankind. There was a mess of a time; no order, no church and people were afraid to go outside.

This is where most of our folklore comes from.

Flying flying ships in India that's what they were. The land was perplexed; man was overwhelmed and the land became rotten there where pyramids were built for the Gods. Symbols of otherworldly languages were embedded in stones to worship other celestial beings from other words.

Atlantis had connections with other beings in space doing what they please. They had other plans for Earth and wanted to use humans as slaves. We helped them build their pyramids lined up in space to correlate with the Stars and unearthly rituals. When that rain came down, it not only washed away the land, but it also washed away the Angels and UFOs.

They didn't justleave; they went underground. After the flood, mankind has been under constant watch by the heavens to protect and cherish us so we grow through the century and learn through our trials and tribulations. Until the end of days when they will come from the Earth and reclaim the lands which were taken from them.

Thats why no UFOs ever landed on the White House's lawn; they know the wrath of God. But now , in my opinion, we're entering into the last days that were started when Israel became a country again.

UFOs explosions have been taking place since then; God is gearing up to come back again and before that happens many things have to come forth that have been living underneath our feet, waiting for their moment.

But back to the topic at hand, every culture from the old world, even in paintings has flying objects. Even in caves, there are drawings of flying objects. Let's go back in time to when there was complete darkness.

God came and said, "Let there be light and He is still going and growing throughout the universe."

His voice echoes through the darkness creating galaxies, Suns, and planets that still exist today. The universe is still expanding through the explosions of God's powerful voice echoing in the darkness.

We call it the Big Bang theory; how ironic.

The Big Bang is God's voice echoing through the universe. Every Galaxy commands what Stars are in existence like a chain of command. Every Star which has a Sun commands the planets and the planets command the moons. Every planet has a certain amount of life is dictated to it as a gift from the heavens.

There are many Earths out there; scientists have proven that there are up to 15 Earth-like planets in other galaxies alone. Now let's go back and talk about these UFOs and so-called aliens. They were running out of here by God's divine power. Remember he said, "He is the Lord of Lords, King of Kings and God of God's." That's why he stated that he rules the universe. These so-called aliens are now coming back because they're allowed to.

I must give you another story about a year ago.

While watching a pastor preaching on TV, I could have screamed and thrown my shoe at the screen. The pastor stated that, "God created all of us and one day we'll all have a planet to rule."

This was insinuating that God basically made only us as a homosapien.

How cocky mankind can be sometimes. To think and have and the notion that God only created us;it sounds good. The Vatican has hidden in their archives the secret of the UFOs and Aliens. They feel that we are not ready for the truth so they hide clues, hinting at it in all our movies.

The truth has a way to go through movies from deep thoughts in our brains. It is funny the Bible does not talk about UFOs or aliens and Christians won't accept UFOs or aliens but they're here. Christians won't accept that there is life other than us but the truth is coming soon, very soon.

Muslims, too, believe in a Genie which can be interpreted as an other worldly creature. In Iraq there were stories of our soldiers shooting at a Genie; they saw things on the radar but there was nothing when they looked with their own eyes.

There is a story of our soldiers fighting against a Giant. I was reading that there been over six hundred UFO cases worldwide. There been cases where kids where playing on a playground and a ship came down and showed itself three days in row and then we have Christians who're stuck, only in the belief that God created just us.

Some UFOs and some aliens want to enslave us; some would like to take over our Earth. God will allow that because He is the ruler, He is our savior and someday He will be their savior. UFOs and aliens have done what they want for so long that they feel that they are celestial and they are the Gods, Lords and rulers of the Universe.

One day all will bow as one to the Al-Mighty God and the Creator. I cannot tell you what's the agenda of the UFOs and the aliens. They have been around for a long time and they are not going anywhere. They have studied us, messed with our DNA and God is watching. The Angels have kept watch over man's progress.

I cannot even tell you how many UFOs and aliens are out there but there's probably more than we can imagine. Just like we have so many planets and galaxies out there and we don't know. You have a right to believe what you want but Earth was flat at one time, right?

I know we are looking at galaxies through Hubble and we observe was truly remarkable. You know the Russians had a book that leaked out the names of different races like us from other galaxies with their names and locations in the star system of UFOs and aliens. The public is not ready to know, see and observe, these things but you can't erase God from our history. I studied electronics in the 80s; it's amazing to leap in electronics instruments.

You ask yourself; how did we go from vacuum tube to a transistors?

Or we went from parallel and series circuits to small integrated circuits the size of a bug, incredible. I studied this stuff in 1982. Then out of high school I worked for the Allied Signal and we helped make the circuit boards to make a plane fly around the world on one tank of gas. I was in school when Reagan put the satellites in space, in the Star Wars project.

I knew instantly what the target was for and why.

So, we could feel safe from any outside threats. Almost every agent society on Earth has had some sort of interaction with the UFOs and aliens but people still believe they don't exist. I must convey the story that I have told many about.

In the late eighties I was driving to 7-Eleven in Kansas City Kansas. What I pulled and in 7-Eleven there where about a hundred people standing around in and out of their cars. My first thought from being in a neighborhood like that was that somebody had gotten shot and killed during a drug deal.

So, I went into the 7-Eleven. I always love to get chocolate milk and coconut donuts. This girl was the checker.

As I was paying for everything, I asked, "What happened here?"

She told me, "You must have just missed it. A huge flying saucer disc was over the building."

Her eyes were big, you would think as if she saw a ghost. I chuckled and laughed as I walked out with my chocolate milk and donuts. Then later that day I saw a friend of mines brother. He told me before work while smoking a cigarette that he watched a silver disc in the sky sitting there for 20 minutes.

Mind you, this area was mostly all African Americans. In the late 80s, this was a day when the sky was bright and blue that day with hardly any clouds; there couldn't be two people mistaken about what they might have seen.

So I got home and the next day I look at a newspaper. The headline read that *"10,000 people from Kansas City, Kansas, called in to the police department to make complaints of a giant flying saucer over the city."*

Spotting something like this in broad daylight, it's not like the Phoenix lights but it had an effect on the people. They are here and they're not going anywhere any time soon. UFOs and aliens have always been among us. But I repeat to mankind, they're not your God or Lords. Just other types of people that were created in the universe and God made us all.

My brother, the middle one, who's been through so much, now loves God. I think through prayer he is still alive. Once, he came to me in private, on Christmas day and started telling me a story of when he was in his backyard one night.

This thing jumped his fence and it looked like a creature with big eyes and a big head. He stated at me and then started to run. Whatever it was, it was agile, fast and quick. It jumped the fence and ran across the yard, jumped the neighbors fence and so on.

Then he stated to me in private, that he saw this creature because he lives close two Bendix, a private Government facility.

He knew that I believed in others in the universe, that's why he came to me in private. There is no telling how many private stories like that exist and those like my brother who will never speak of it again. UFOs will be in our lives for a long time to come and in the future.

They are now a part of our culture. They are in all the movies and it seems like, if nothing else, we are being socially prepared for this Awakening. They are in our skies; they are underneath the ground and they have been here since God cleansed the Earth and beyond. They are slowly resurfacing in our lives.

If you take fluorescent lights of different colors and make high pitch musical sounds in a remote location, you might be able to see them but it's not always a good thing or it turns out well. They have been here for a long time in the shadows and many of them call this home, how ironic.

The Christian faith calls them demonic; they are not all demonic but another form of God's creation. But that doesn't mean that they're benevolent and they're not deceitful and they won't lie and say they created us.

God created you and things in the universe and all the things around you and all the heavens.

VIII

PURPOSE OF SOULS

The purpose of souls is to help other souls through the transition of life and death. Yet all are essential in experience to become better in growth to obtain closeness to our creator. I remember my grandmother told me a story about a dream she had about the day she died, and she saw all her relatives floating down a river in a boat in which her mom was with their father and cousins, and they slowed down the boat.

Then, they laid out a ramp and said, "Come on, girl, join us. Your time has come and gone." She told them to continue, and that she was not done yet. She continued to have that dream into her 90s, and I assume she eventually joined them all on that boat. Her time has come and gone.

Why did she tell me this story? Also, why would I tell you this story? Because when you were born into this world, before you come you know there's going to be a pain, that's told to you. Before you're born into this world, you know there are going to be good times and bad times. That is inevitable, and there is exhortation before entering the physical world.

It's funny, something just whispered into my ear. Everyone promises to make a change in the physical world before they are born into the womb. What a promise we all have given. Each of us is born into a certain family, a certain race, certain group to make better, not worse. Yet we come to find, most likely through the seed of Adam and Eve, that we end up doing bad, even though our hearts mean good.

Back to my grandmother's story: that story is conveyed because the purpose of a soul in your ancestry when you die is to welcome you back to where you came from, to help console the pain we just endured in the life of the physical. Everyone, every soul on Earth right now, had a choice not to come.

I remember when my kids were small, they used to say "I'm going to have this car, this big house, I'm going to be famous. I am going to have much more than what you have, Dad."

I would just laugh because as a kid, I had many dreams to be better than my parents, but the path life offers don't always work out. I planned to be the best running back the NFL ever saw, but things happened to alter those plans.

We do the same before we enter the womb. We boast about how we're going to change things down there on the tiny, blue planet called Earth, in the Milky Way galaxy. And yet, we still have sins, bountiful in our world, and when we die, we have suffered much and have many scars on our own souls.

An alcoholic raises an alcoholic, a pedophile raises a pedophile, a drug dealer raises a drug dealer, and so on. Even though all of us have promised to make better, the one who did was Jesus Christ, who fulfilled his promise in so many ways that it's the light that still shines on Earth. But when you die, the souls before you will be there, waiting for you with many hugs of love and compassion. That's their job.

One time, I yelled at God. This was in the '90s I said, "All these drugs, all this killing. I cannot help my people. You brought me here to help my people. Everything I try, it's blocked somehow. I try everything to help, but the enemy wins. Where is my help? When I said I wanted to kill people, you blocked me from doing that. Now, I owe you the favor, God, for changing me. I like to help those to convince them not to kill like God did for me, but I don't have the tools I need to help others."

He told me it was not my time yet.

"Your time will come when I make use of you as a tool," he said.

Then he showed me a vision of heaven. I was standing with a bunch of souls, crying, and as I looked around, they had scars, blood, and deep wounds that life had given them on Earth, and they were all worshipping the glorious light in the heavenly sky.

That vision still stays with me today. There was none—I mean, none—I saw in this vision without a blemish on their souls. Even Jesus has blemishes from the nails of the cross in his hands.

Earth receives us, beautiful as a baby coming out of the womb. In the end, when we die, we are covered in some sort of pain from life in the physical world. When you die, the souls welcome you. They wash your body and put a robe on you. I remember going to Hawaii, and when I got off the plane, they greeted us with a lei.

They welcome you to the island in the same way once you die. They welcome you back home. The thing that makes Jesus so great was not just the works he did down here. Before his soul was put into a woman's womb, he promised and did what he promised in saving the world.

Many before him before entering a woman's womb didn't fulfill what they promised in saving and helping the world to become a better place. That's a new direction of love, compassion, and having a relationship with our Father in heaven. So, that is huge to promise before entering the womb to Earth.

Then, living on earth, maintaining that promise, and then dying for our sins and being resurrected, showing us that through Him, we can receive salvation and a personal relationship with God in the flesh, to always be able to call upon his name on earthly bound, is a miracle.

So, back to the saints in heaven. Their job is to welcome and prepare souls coming, in leaving spiritual mental guidance for those who are afraid to come back to the physical world, and those who just left it. I remember asking God, "What do you do to those who are intoxicated or inebriated because they are still drunk or high, not realizing that they're dead and their spirit is in another place?"

What a weird question, huh? The answer was simple. The saints handle that and wait till they sober up, because they're not going anywhere else no time soon. Another thing that saints do in heaven is coordinate the services, like on Earth. Certain singers want to have concerts, and they have orchestras with many instruments we have not seen or heard of on Earth. The saints preside over festivals and games being played. There are songs in heaven that are never heard down here.

A saint or soul also regulates themselves, so if negativity begins, they try to nip it in the bud. There is praise, holding hands up to the heavenly sky, and worshipping God, which definitely comes first. But souls also have an obligation to make it sweeter for those coming and going.

It's similar to the way there are churches down here but on a much broader scale. There will be many testimonies. There will be people playing instruments everywhere, singing all the time, holding hands, and loving each other, like a breath of fresh air.

Remember, everything you see down here is but a replica of the real thing in heaven. That is a prophecy to those leaving for the physical world. They're also crying for those returning from the physical world, but they'll praise the Almighty God.

IX

SOULS IN HEAVEN

S ouls in heaven what a beautiful thing. We think has heaven being a place of beauty and hope and love that's secret and mystical of all the places we can imagine in our thoughts and mind. It has many colors with various animals and flying birds and among others, in complete harmony of giving God all the praise. There's always singing music playing to the tune which gives God all the glory. The light from the sky that hits your heavenly face is God's Glory from the throne above it is truly all that and more.

You ask how can I get to this perpetuating place saturated with love?

Where you see so much, that not a church of Churches can compare to this singing and the sight.

Is it an illusion to your soul and mind?

Magical is what it is.

When you walk through the gates you are naked again where there singing birds flying, a robe to cover your naked body. The Gate itself is captivating, made of crystal and gold in the finest gems.

As you walk alone through that gate they're singing and praising and welcoming you to your old home where you once live you don't remember. Many fall to their knees as Jesus is waiting there to hug them.

To welcome you back to this place that's compelling with perpetuating love and harmony and peace.

No distortion, no lies, truth with praise and harmony.

You say why would someone leave such a place?

As captivating and compelling filled with so much love I could worship God forever in such a place.

By the way before, I answer that question, there are these particular souls. They are draped in gold robes, in which they are very noticeable, throughout the heavens. These Souls are chosen to never leave heaven always devoted to giving God praise in the Heavenly Realm. They sound different than everyone and they walk differently it's kind of comical in a way like they are the nerds in heaven but highly respected and loved because they would never betray the Heavenly Father.

Now back to the question?

Why would a soul leave such a glorious place?

That's why I mentioned the nerdy souls draped in gold they never get tired of worshipping the heavenly father. But on the other hand, there are souls who for thousands of years begin to want something different. After so long praising God, God learned that His creation gets tired of the routine of giving Him the glory and praise so they sought to go back into the war zone.

The best Earthly way I can explain it's like a soldier going back to war in Iran on his fourth tour or a man who just gets out of jail and wants to go right back in. I guess you can call it being physically institutionalized. You would think on a rational level or spiritual level no one could conceive to leave but Souls do all the time.

When God told me this I could have cried because now I am here, the one who left Him. I have chosen to not worship Him for thousands of yearswhich when He truly deserves and much more. I say, "I love you, Father. It'sglory withinitself."

So I know you are starting to catch on to why there is a physical ramification.

The physical ramifications of what's God made were merely to satisfy the souls who got tired of routine worship in Heaven so God left heaven in the mist at the darkness and yelled out, "Let there be light."

His voice continues to echo through the darkness creating vast solar systems with many galaxies, stars, and moons. Heaven is divine and has it in all its array of beauty.

Unfortunately, there have been a number of souls wanting to leave to experience the physical realm. Many angels cast out of heaven because of their desire to be on Earth. We think Lucifer was the last to turn on God but there have been others besides him that tried to create a dreadful war.

Despite all the praise, all the singing and all the love and beauty, heaven has had its fill of pain also.

So God left heaven in the midst of His creation to have a relationship with the two being that He created from mud. So, Earth would be like Heaven and literally, all hell broke loose in Heaven and Lucifer betrayed God and the war in Heaven began.

It's something that hurts God's heart and makes my heart hurt. There have been several times we have made God's heart hurt.

The great flood made God's heart hurt, Sodom and Gomorrah and also the crucifixion of His son God's heart hurt. But nevertheless, he still loves us through all the heartache.

Now through all that let's go back after you leave the physical realm and go through those gates of Heaven and past the test the birds fly down to give you your robe of glory I didn't mention that Jesus commends you by putting on your robe of glory which is made of all the metals you earned on your physical journey to return with the scars that you endured just like Jesus still has his scars from what he endured.

Now, wait there is one more thing to talk about.

How to make it past those beautiful gates to receive this glorious place.

When come up to to receive there is a book not per se based on your sins but based on your interactions with God. It's a book that this tall spirit next to God is holding – it's your book of Life. You should see how you start trembling with fear but you can hear the singing whichbrings some ease to the Souls.

This tall spirit next to God opens your book of Life and talks about your interaction with God how you talk to Him and praise Him in the physical realm. You accept his son as the world's savior.

However, if you don't know those things, then the book is blank. It's when God gives us another chance to go out and do better. Fill the pages of the book so that when you return, God doesn't turn you away.

I won't state that there is a hell that's not my concern but my concern is to help you pass through those gates into that glorious singing. Talk to God please and let Him know who you are, so you won't be trembling when your book is opened. He will know how many times you welcomed Him into your home. The tall soul reads the book and calls out your birth name as you come forth to be presented.

Like a grim reaper, he has no smile, no emotion, his garment is grey like the cloudy sky. When he picks up your book it is a good sign. That means you spent time talking to God, having a full relationship and He knows your voice. He knows there is a loving relationship and God loves that.

If you want to reach that heavenly realm, you must make time to talk in solitude so you can be one of the souls in Heaven, singing and flying around enjoying worshipping Him.

There are no planes or cars in heaven.

Heaven is not small by any means.

Can you imagine flying next to a beautiful flock of birds and heaven?

We all were once there, how beautiful, right?

You say why can't remember any of this beautiful place so call heaven?

When souls enter the womb, the water in the womb of a woman has certain enzymes that erases your memory of heaven.

By the way, the transition to fully being on Earth takes a couple of years depending on the soul itself.

Do you get what I mean?

If you ever a one-year-old or two-year-old they are still between two worlds, so you can ask them questions there might be still some answers there to help find where they came from. That's why babies can pick up existing souls that are lingering around the Earth but that's a whole other story.

When you read this and you find out you left that glorious place, it might make you wonder , *'What was I thinking?'*

But it's not all bad; many of us feel like we can make Earth a better place.

We took that challenge being blindfolded memories erased and growing up and a household in that you didn't have a choice. We thought it would be easy to reach a place of exalting the Almighty God again.

What a challenge.

Don't you feel so far away sometimes?

In a strange land, I hope to make it back home. I hope this book helps to guide you truly in the direction to being souls in Heaven again with Love, giving God praise.

So, I want you to do your best so that when that tall soul opens your book, it's almost too heavy for him to pick up because you have talked to God in solitude and established a relationship with Him. You will not be trembling with fear when your book is opened and much will be said about you and the Almighty God.

Amen.

X

CONFIRMATION

In this chapter, I have to ask God to give me a confirmation from the Scriptures from the Bible - a sign to let me know that He speaks through me in this book. So, I scrolled through the Old Testament first. Then I went further into the New Testament and God whispered into my ear, I came to the end of the Bible in Revelations, then He told me to read the seven seals.

I got to Chapters 6-13 in Revelations and which stated the stars of heaven fell into Earth. Then I heard a whisper, "Keep reading."

And that caught my attention indeed. So, I kept reading and then I got to Chapters 8-12 verse in Revelations, and my heart almost stopped beating.

It stated, *"The fourth angel sounded, in which is a trumpet for war, and part of the sun was smitten, then it states a third of the moon was smitten and a third part of them was darkened."*

How ironic on Earth, we have videos of strange things looking like giant ships, flying into our sun on YouTube. We heard of our bases on the backside of the moon. We have a video of strange activity out in the stars and here, we have one Scripture in Revelation talking about smiting those areas.

How ironic, right?

If you don't know what smitten means, it means destroyed.

Why would they want to destroy a third part of the moon?

Can anyone on Earth answer that million-dollar question?

Also, why would they destroy a third of the stars in space??

It doesn't make any sense; in these places, we don't have a domain. However, it makes perfect sense. If there are other humanoids out there in the cosmos on the side of the Antichrist, it makes perfect sense. It makes perfect sense if those ships have been flying into our sun taking energy from it.

See the Antichrist is not by himself. He has Allies throughout the cosmos. These Allies are the ones who lived in Atlantis, the very same city that God sank to the bottom of the sea during the great flood. There is no need to keep searching for Atlantis. God took care of that.

The Allies of the Antichrist changed the appearance of mankind like the Nordics who made man blond and blue-eyed. Like the Asian race which was also changed. I know that statement probably will make people mad and upset but the aliens, these allies of the Antichrist, have broken rules in the development of mankind.

This all started in heaven a long time ago when Satan vowed to harm mankind. Even the Angels changed us into giants; the Nepheline was by design and plan. Even the African race has been tampered with the likes of the pygmies, a small group of people in the jungle. Cold and hot regions of the world can change us to adapt to the region.

But I am no scientist but I think our DNA has been tampered with and when Jesus comes back, they will all be dealt with. So those of you who believe that the humanoids have created us, I don't think so. It's a lie they convey to us through the powers that be.

Some of our leaders have been tricked by the Allies of the Antichrist, allowing them to obtain technically that we enjoy today like integrated circuits, cell phones, etc. They have broken the laws of God in space and they will be dealt with for tampering with our DNA giving out the technology before its time.

They are not your Gods and proven soon in the last days, there will be a clash of worlds, the physical and the spiritual. It's already beginning now. Their penalty is their sun will be blackened.

You see, my God does not fly around in ships. He makes Suns in the midst of the darkness by saying *"Let there be light."*

My God doesn't die when He crashes in New Mexico from the Roswell crash. My God makes planets by speaking them into existence. My God made all the heavens and the Earth by the sound of His glorious voice and those humanoids who hide in the Earth and sin against God and man will be smitten on the backside of the moon. The star that God has made will fall upon the Earth.

In Chapters 8-11 they even name one of the fallen smitten stars called Wormwood. The star in which is a sun will be blackened like night and glory will be totally restored to the Real Creator of all, the Almighty God Himself….. You.

XI

ATHEISM

I don't know why but the idea of God being a jealous God spoke to me.

On the topic of atheism, I once thought the same thing—that there's no God because of all the evil going on in the world. It seems in our day and time that evil always wins the race. In the midst of good, love, and compassion, evil always comes to steal that glory.

A beautiful child gets hit by a car and passes away; there is no God. A young man falls in love, and it starts off nice and beautiful, but he goes off to war and never comes back; there's no God. Someone loses their job and goes off and kills 19 people; there's no God.

In another type of incident, someone gets abducted by U.F.O.; there is no God. Someone sees a giant U.F.O. flashing like the Phoenix lights; there is no God. Somewhere else, a person believes in Satanic things like witchcraft or worshipping Satan; there is no God.

There are thousands of reasons not to believe in God. Some believe in ancient texts from the old world—the Anunnaki.

In all these scenarios, can they take you away from the Creator? If the answer for that is going to Walmart and buying a brand-new Ouija board, then yes. I know it sounds like a joke but not believing in God is not a joke. With this board, you will get evil demonic things in your home and around your family. It's dangerous and reckless, it will cause certain portals to open, but only God can save you once you go down that path. We see evil possession movies, and 90% of them are true because someone chooses the evil path instead of a good path and their family and loved ones have to pay the price. I know I had these discussions with God, asking why does it take so long?

The thing is evil moves so fast. This is why he wanted me to bring up atheism by the answer he gave to me to tell you. It isn't as if I was slow and that evil is fast. Evil begets evil it has only one purpose. Evil means not answering prayers and changing lives, displaying love, and seeing the beautiful end result with harmony and compassion.

Anything is harder to build than to tear down, and evil tears down, so it seems like God is working slower. We are built to be apart from him; we are not complete without him, so when things go wrong, the first one we blame is him. Evil has only one purpose, which is to destroy everything God has.

That's no excuse for God; He could stop evil, but He gave us a choice, and that choice sometime breeds evil. That's not God's fault. So, would you not want God to give us choices? Personally, I would prefer to have some choices. And if I fail in my choices, may I pay the price?

It's not God committing this evil; we create evil in the physical and in the non-physical, Earthly and non-Earthly. Then, we blame Him for it. We live in a progressively evil world made up of many evil choices, and God gave us choices. We know what good is, we know what righteousness is, and we know God gave His son to save us, but yet we find a way, a loophole through choice to seek evil over good. Evil affects us in that we choose another over Him and say He doesn't exist anymore to say our behavior isn't that wrong.

Amen.

XII

END OF DAYS

Years ago, I was in my room seeking the Creator, trying to sift every inch of Him. In a private setting, inclusive, no disturbance to finding and defining what's real about this God of ours. If real, He is gonna talk to me, and prove Himself right, or don't waste my time and effort. I want to seek valuable information to justify any actions to call Him the Lord of Lords and Kings of Kings.

I challenged Him to prove His existence; prove the right to be called God of Gods. Now mind you in my life I've been around many liars and mini-perpetrators, I wasn't ready to tolerate being swindled by no one.

So in my newness, God shot down in our loneliness, together for countless hours, showing me a vision of the future. A future in which I saw Jesus coming through the clouds to take back the lands which were lost on the small planet Earth. But in the vision do know what was beside my feet, right next to me?

You'll never guess in a thousand years - it was a flying saucer pierced in the dirt. In the 1980s, could you imagine seeing such a vision as a 17-year-old kid?

If I would have told anyone about this vision they would have laughed and had me committed. But now all these years later will anyone actually laugh?

Maybe because we can see such things unraveling so slowly through movies, the internet, etc. Now, back then in this vision, I asked God, "Why am I standing next to a flying saucer?"

He answered, "Every Antichrist that tries to overcome Earth has been assisted by outside sources who claimed to be celestial beings for mankind."

So, I began to watch and study UFO shows and see how gradually over the years they intertwined themselves in our culture and in our movies, and on the internet. They show off their technology, causing small waves, giving us technology in bits and pieces at a time.

So, after looking to my left and seeing this flying saucer pierced in the dirt, I looked to my right and saw a man with his back arched looking up to the sky with his arms out, shooting electrical current out of his hands toward Jesus Christ, our Savior. I could not see his face, his back was turned toward me.

He had an expensive gray suit on with black shiny shoes and was very well-dressed. Then I looked up towards Jesus in the sky and to his right, flying towards him were jets in the sky, fighting against Jesus Christ our Savior. So, you have jets and a man in a dress suit shooting electrical current up to Jesus and flying saucers from another world trying to overcome the one who died for us on the cross. How sad.

This is the vision that has been embedded in my head for many years and I have not told many to not seem crazy or delusional. But in turn, I felt it was just a dream but now so many years later, I can't help wondering, is it really?

We have aliens and cartoons, and every other movie. If you went and Googled, "How many aliens movies we have had in the last 10 years?" you'll be shocked. We are being prepared slowly for this new Awakening. The Antichrist is not alone just like Napoleon and Hitler were not alone. Some say Hitler had flying saucers, look it up.

So now in this present day, I don't feel so idiotic about this vision and it lets me know that God is real, day by day. Back then I did not know what that vision entailed but now I know. Sometimes life is a teacher, only wishing to show us enlightenment, to finally understand

God, our Creator. It took me 40 years to understand that vision and now I see a dark light at the end of that tunnel.

I have read recently that some believe we were created by aliens. That's the LIE that is going to lead us to make that vision come true. There are ships flying through space right now, coming here to either defy or not defy Jesus coming back to claim the lands. But we don't need Jesus to come back if we now have a body of people who open our minds to sift for God's presence in our lives to take back our Earth physically and spiritually by putting God first in our lives and our families.

God granted us telepathy to read minds, to float in the air, and to walk across the water to put these evil spirits in check that roam around us and latch on to us to cause us to create such malicious acts. The end of the days will cause a war on Earth that we never encountered or witnessed. Before we can change, we need to get stronger through His grace and power.

Weed out segregation and the church and open your mind to the threats in the outside world. The only way to combat that threat is by having God's power running through your veins. I felt that power in the 80s and it scared me and others but you can now take up that cross and become a vessel of Hope, not seeking Jesus to return to have this end of days. We can save ourselves, wipe that vision away; it's a terrible vision to see and to put Jesus in that position because we can't save ourselves just by a commitment to the almighty God.

The church has given up on mankind; it's waiting for the rapture when it should be seeking God's grace and power to take control of the world in which we live. You receive God's five spiritual gifts to become a soldier for mankind to survive all the adversities in the physical realm.

Bring heaven on Earth.

That vision of Jesus coming through the clouds was beautiful and sad at the same time to see; others trying to destroy him and destroy mankind is a sad vision to behold and endure as a young man at that time. I know we can do better but it has to start with one for the hope of mankind.

After hearing about this vision, do you still choose to close your eyes?

In 2020, I saw on the news that another tape from the Pentagon had been released of a US pilot chasing an unidentified object.

The church says this is demonic and it doesn't exist in the physical realm, but then what was that?

These are other humanoids and they're here to enslave you, to cause you to think that they are celestial beings. Some are good and some are bad but wake up and smell the coffee - a war is about to take place. We are not in the physical or spiritual realm anymore. People will begin to stop believing in God when seeing these objects from space.

The church is under threat right now through diseases and other outside sources. In the end of days, things will start coming out of the ground and the ocean. Spirits will show themselves in battle, bullets flying, missiles flying; dust and dirt everywhere and people crying. The carnage will be like what you'd see in a video game but this is really happening. What a horrible sight for all to see.

I believe Jesus will prevail in the end.

Unfortunately, I did see that vision but it's your job to obtain the answer to the rest of the vision through your relationship with the Almighty God. Evil spirits will be jumping in people's bodies to fight against Jesus. These spirits will be jumping into pilots to shoot missiles at God. It's an all-out war but Jesus has always said, "Vengeance is mine."

The Lord said, "I shall not show any mercy, I shall not stray away from what I have come to do and claim the right of being the Messiah of all. As the Messiah, I raise my sword against those who choose not to believe in my father and harmony. Have mercy and love to appreciate all that He has created.

My sword, ear-piercing voice of power wards off any evil. The universe and the heavens will know my name, the great Messiah of the world and the worlds to come. My robe has the anointing of God's power on it to glisten through all the smoke and fire that was bestowed upon me from those who choose not to believe.

To those who choose to fire their weapons upon the great Messiah now see my might and bow down and beg for mercy. They should say we beseech you Lord we have mistaken and underestimated thy Almighty power.

They who came from the ocean, they who crawled out of their holes, they who come from afar in the skies, they will try to escape me and crawl back into the holes attack should not happen. They who come from the heavens will try to get back in their ships and leave and that shall not happen. They who come from the ocean and try to go back and swim away that should not happen.

They shall think that they can escape and one day regroup to affect mankind again - that shall not happen. They will be judged and bound to reap the repercussions of their actions to try to come against the almighty Messiah.

Those who did not believe that I was the Messiah the first time who bowed down to their knees and worshipped my father and I as the victors of Earth to bring back the lands in which it was supposed to be, I will teach man how to be like me and I will give him the keys to travel the universe to spread my word across the Galaxies.

After this victory on Earth, many shall tell the story from sunup to sundown. In the midst of such darkness on Earth, a light came from the clouds. Seeking victory in the midst of a dark Earth and what's now heaviness come to save us once again. We want to be saved from the flood and the fire.

In my sword Glory and my voice of might no one will deny who I am. No one would defy me that's being the Almighty Messiah. The one who was crucified as a lamb, who shed his blood on the cross for the sake of mankind to become closer to the almighty Father. My robe has smoke coming from it from all the weapons trying to destroy me but I don't have a scratch.

The first time I allowed those to beat me, spit on me and to ridicule me. But this time, I am not the one to be ridiculed, they will be the ones who beg for mercy. After the victory and my robe still smokes I will preach to all nations; they shall hear in their own tongues to understand me. To worship and lift their hands to ask forgiveness for going against the almighty Messiah.

The weapons that engage against my skin, the more anointing they saw. Seeing the radiance from my face, some dropped their weapons and dropped to their knees in prayer. I beseech you Lord to forgive me, remember my name."

How amazing in the midst of battle, to give up and worship, in the heart of the battle to accept defeat. But the enemies' eyes were filled with the anointing of Jesus' face as the bullets hit him.

I don't know if I have sufficiently explained in this chapter how incredible it can feel to have God give me this opportunity to share with you. He is the love of my life. My secret to you is this gift, whether you believe in it or not, I lift my hands to worship right now in every way through my body and soul.

I pray that everyone except this book to him better in all glory.

Amen.

XIII

AFTERMATH

Aftermath is when Heaven is now on Earth and then we back to God's teaching in one accord in alignment with His goal for us towards the future. The war of the world is over when people on Earth see that God exists and He is real; no doubts and no confusion. That means Heaven on Earth through divine intervention.

Everyone on the planet knows where we came from and also who created us and why. People believe Heaven is coming down to Earth; no that's not the case. Heaven coming is God's presence roaming the streets with people seeking His higher power.

You say why would people seek God's higher power?

I am about to get to that in a moment.

Earth will still has its share of problems, of course. People will be roaming the streets seeking God's attention. There won't be any begging for people to talk to God on a daily basis. They will be yearning for His attention to be fed to gain His wisdom.

You say why the sudden change?

Because Jesus returned and captivated the Earth.

But the biggest change is the power certainty one will have heaven on Earth like Jesus. God gave me a vision of a young child about seven leaving school with his mom in the morning and seeing the next-door neighbor floating in the air with his eyes closed, and legs folded, meditating like you see in the Star Wars movie.

The child says, "Look mommy, I want to be like that one day."

The movement is incredible just like everyone in the Star Wars movie seeking out the force. God is the force isn't that amazing? Man is always a hair-off in his thinking.

When you see the amazing monks doing unbelievable things you will see people in robes seeking the five steps I talked about in chapter 1. You have five senses that you were born with that would be five spiritual senses that you meditate to receive gifts from God such as levitation, also skipping across water, healing the sick, having remarkable wisdom, lifting amazing objects, and reading minds to not be deceived by no one.

When you see these Chosen ones walking down the street with the force, God's Force, they are more revered. He has made them more honorable than any soldier. In fact, they are soldiers of God to be ambassadors to go out into the cosmos and preach God's word.

We went through all this pain in history which could have been avoided if Eve wouldn't have eaten that apple. The entire Earth is now like the garden of Eden. Like you see in the Star Wars movie, kids want to be Jedi and have the force. That's just how it will be on Earth.

I remember the first Star Wars movie I watched, I thought it was the most stupid movie I have ever seen but people loved it; I don't know why or they don't know either but it's the most popular movie ever in my opinion. The amazing God has ways of showing us things and we don't even know he's there talking to us.

I now appreciate the Star Wars movies because they show us the aftermath of the end of days, and of us being God's ambassador in space throughout the cosmos. God has a right to speak through anyone just as he spoke to a whale to swallow up Jonah. He spoke to George Lucas to bring us Star Wars.

I know there's going to be those we're going to say, "God spoke this to you?"

"Well, he spoke to a whale so he can speak through me."

He can also speak to you through any of us. I am not special like I said in chapter 1; I am dust underneath the feet. Sometimes I wish I wouldn't have gotten afraid in the eighties and sought out all of God's five gifts in the spirit. I know in my fifties I will be able to levitate in the air, skip across the water but I guess the world wasn't ready for that at that time so I bow down to the times at hand.

I heard there was a guy in Africa has some of the gifts from God and they tried to kill him numerous times and they failed. But he eventually disappeared.

Could you imagine what would have happened to me if I wrote this book in the 80s?

They would have had me committed.

So, I've been waiting in silence all these years. To tell this story of God's plan for man. The garden of Eden, God's Spirit teaching us, still has to go on, we just went the roundabout way. I believe now society is ready for enlightenment.

Through many stories and all the rumors of wars and all the pain we went through, man on Earth is ready right now. Ready to accept this book now in time to see into the future he was made with God. He has also used me as His tool to convey His message. I am used as a tool; I am not here to fight against the church or fight against the Bible or fight against other people's opinions.

If you feel disrespect for your religion or your opinions or your relationship with God, talk to God about it. Maybe you received the same message I have received and you will be used as a tool also. If you say this is fiction and entertainment that's fine also but time will tell if in fact, this is fiction.

I do not do this for glorification for myself but glorification of the Maker and your relationship to grow and be stronger with Him and only Him. There is another subject that God told me about, that is disturbing to me as it brings pain to my heart. I can feel the pain and sorrow underneath my feet and in the skies above. It's starting and it's going to be a great problem in the future. In the aftermath, there is hybrid breeding in the heavens above.

There is slavery developing in the cosmos. Evil is growing in space now. Jesus has to come back soon not just for our sake but for others in the cosmos so heaven can be on Earth. Only then can we begin our training to go into the cosmos as warriors of God to break those who worship other Gods, to let them know who created us and them and His love, to feel the void and their cup which is empty will now be filled.

Humans have been getting abducted for many years and this makes me angry. Earth people must train soon to overcome this growing threat underneath my feet and above is very sad. The same type of creatures that were made pre-flood in the Bible are being made now in the heavens and underneath my feet.

The agenda is still there and still in thought. There are always those in the heavens who seek empowerment over others for personal gain. It makes me upset that the church calls the other forms of humanoids demonic creatures. Demonic creatures don't fly around in spaceships.

It doesn't work that way.

Demonic creatures are in the spiritual realm not in spaceships. In the future, I can tell you they will need the Gospel also. We are crusaders of God tasked to convey that message on a daily basis. They contend that they are smarter than we are so why should they listen?

As humans we have dealt with warfare on Earth, personally witnessing the battle between good and bad. Jesus had to come down and in that spiritual warfare so his might power and goodness. No humanoid in space is smarter than God; none has yelled out His voice and planets, stars, and galaxies were created; none displayed such intelligence and reverence.

There was darkness now there is light. How shall you, a slave and hybrid, use this to commit crimes against God?

I am a descendant of slavery saw the effects from being an Afro-American on Earth, the remnants of slavery being in the cosmos. It seems like the future and history through all the humanoids we keep on making the same stupid mistakes. I pray that this part of the book is fiction, not truth that I am wrong, and that what I am feeling above and beneath my feet is truly false.

I remember when I was in college I met a black lady and we talked about God. I started telling her something and she didn't freak out but she brought another older black woman to meet me in college; her wisdom was over the top. Her hands were soft, and when she touched my face, I felt her anointing.

"There he is," the other one said to her. She touched my face and immediately started praying. Others walked around us going to class, crazy, right?

"You are chosen by God and you will one day have a story to tell," she told me.

I wonder if it is that day now? I feel blessed to be that dirty old wrench, to be used by God to give you all valuable information to the world. To be chosen or not to be chosen by God is in the hands of the beholder who read this book.

All I can do is hope, one day, you seek God's reverence and define glory. I have felt God's anointing; there's no drug on Earth compared to it. I want you to seek God's power in your brain to become the most powerful monk that the world has ever seen.

Have the Force like a Star Wars but it's God's Force. God bless Earth and the cosmos so that they will be saved under His goodness.

Amen.

The thing is Christians in this age want to be more powerful. But in the aftermath, they are not by any means second in stepping up to the plate with ideas to make mankind stronger on the Earth and beyond.

They are leaders and soldiers for God when they walk into a room their presence is recognized. People will seek to be like the Godly soldiers and seek God out because of them and you shall have the gifts by his grace and power.

This time now Christians don't have this power but in the future, that won't be the case. We now have a space force but they are not like the soldiers of God, preaching God's word throughout the universe. Yes, the space force is around but they want to capture and captivate a room like God's soldiers. Just like in Star Wars the one who has the Force but God's force in the future is a specimen to see and admire.

Some many will want to be a part it but they are chosen through their work and the commitment; they give to the Almighty God. You are a monk for mankind is behind schedule we must begin to receive the keys to preach to the heavens; there are souls in space ready to hear the gospel of God but their intelligence is very high so we have to begin our training to show other humanoids the gifts God has or will give us.

They will respect our gifts and our training but Jesus must give us the keys to space and time. He will say, "Go, sons of man. Go tell the universe of me and my father and the love we have."

It will be a beautiful sight to see and enjoy watching the seed of Adam and Eve in space preaching God's benevolence with anointing and power.

Year One
SATAN'S REIGN. RAVISHING BEAUTY.

Your first year will be a year in which a new savior will have risen. His skin will be golden, not like the brass possessed by Jesus. This savior will be tall, and when he speaks, everyone will listen because of his wisdom and knowledge. Looking into his face will be pleasant, and everyone will gaze upon his presence and beauty. All will love him in his first year; he will come forth as the savior who stops mankind from destroying itself with greed and conquering ways. He will promise peace and love, and harmony. With him, no more will there be nations trying to kill each other with their powers. He will be the new unity and face of Earth.

When he stands, nations shall go up against him, and no man dares to defy him; he has not shown any of his powers but his raw talent of wisdom in bringing nations together in peace. His physique will be perfect, his skin ravishing, his eyes binding, and his walk captivating—because it will encite other men to want to walk like him. His smile will make the room light up. All the supermodels will want to be with him.

The savior is without blemish—whether of the flesh or the spirit. He has stopped nations from fighting like China, the US, Russia, and Iran. When the whole world was at war, he alone came in as a savior with love, peace, beauty, and harmony.

Every nation will honor him this first year. It will be a year of love, beauty, and the discussion of repairing what has been broken.

A third of the world has been destroyed; now Christ has come to save us from total annihilation. He is King of Kings; he is now Lord of Lords—a ravishing beauty. Who can hate him? Who can defy him? He is pure beauty and love. His house will be built on a hill for all to see. He will have a desirable physique, standing tall at just the right height. He will always dress well and strut out on the balcony to gaze at those beneath him as if they are his children.

To those who look upon him, he will say, "Give me thy praise. Am I not the most beautiful man you have ever seen? There is not a woman on Earth that will not make love to me. There's not a man on Earth. That would not want to be me. I am beautiful; exalt me, yes. Praise me, and love me."

To add icing to the cake, he will sing like no other with a voice so captivating, like the choir in heaven. He is a perfect man to admire and love and cherish. But yet, through his beauty and excellence, you will see a dark side to him and hints of silence when he speaks to not leave any options in the moments because he can do no wrong and is fully righteous.

The savior will be better than Jesus ever could be in the flesh. Jesus was bronze, but he will be golden. His energy will be captivating, like he never runs out of energy, like he never sleeps and knows he has seven years to his reign of power.

What's more, he will have the prophetic capability to tell others' future and horoscope with an amazing psychic ability, whether it's dealing with matters of wealth, power, or personal affairs. He will be able to tell others about their dead relatives, and what their deceased family is doing. This enlightenment will give him power over others, with healing capabilities that no other has ever seen on the planet. He will be the modern-day Christ for a small moment until you find out his true colors. But this first year, he will be ravished, praised, and beloved, for he is King, and he is Christ.

If Christ is praised on the donkey, the savior will be praised riding through his limousine in his fancy blue suit with a white shirt with three buttons hanging out on his chest. This image of him will show his eloquence and beauty as a man of power who is full of energy, so much so that he will be able to take what the world has given and give them what they need—a true leader saving them from destruction.

A savior will emerge in that first year of this beautiful new Christ. There will be no more economic division between China and America. There will be no more division from superpower to superpower; he will unite us as one nation with the purpose of unity. Leaders will hear him talk about space and time, taking ownership of outer planets, building lavish space stations, ruling the galaxies, never running out of resources, taking other resources, and bringing them back to Earth to make our planet the richest of all. He will promise leaders everlasting life, riches, and happiness; no one shall have pain. He has the knowledge and power to overcome sickness and make us live and reign for a thousand years on Earth.

In his first year, the savior will heal the sick. Many will bow down to him, surrendering full power. People will wait in lines to see him, gaze upon him, they will seek to walk again, see again, hear again, and be healed and cured of their lifelong diseases. He will go to hospitals and cure those who are dying from cancer. He will be Christ for that first year; he will be beauty and perfection for that first year.

He will be God.

Second Year

THE BEGINNING OF THE ALLIANCE

I n the second year, people will be happy, and things will be heavenly on Earth. The King will have been perfect for several years. Their savior, God, will not have shown any imperfections. Blessed will be his name. People will say, "May he forever live and be over us as king Lord and savior."

Then, one moment, everyone will come outside in a panic, and there will be flying ships all over the world, just like Independence day in every city and state or province.

Do you remember when God let it rain for forty days and forty nights and cleansed the world for the first time in Noah? There were angels sleeping with women. Those fallen angels are back, and they have an alliance with extraterrestrials. The antichrist has been busy forming an alliance roaming the galaxies making promises with others like taking DNA for their own purpose and needs. Movies have already prepared us for these times by envisioning us for future events to come.

Nevertheless, people come outside in fear and see this alien presence, not knowing that their new God has an alliance with these extraterrestrials as they roamed through the heavens for several thousand years. The people saw their savior relinquish us from destroying ourselves. Now the savior will speak out publicly to convey that they mean no harm and are our allies for added protection, protecting us in every city and in every Providence, just in case we are under threat of outside or otherworldly threats. Even though some people disagree, they know their savior has been helpful in sustaining the human race, bringing back order and control in so many lives.

So eventually, the ships will come from outside our ramifications. We won't know what they contain in them, but they will become a part of our daily ritual. We will look up, see them, and begin to feel comfortable with them in our skies and feel safe again.

At the same time, we won't know the ships are monitoring everyone's household through zeros and ones—anything that has the digital capability with integrated circuits. The ships will have total control to listen, observe, and report back to our Savior. So if anyone speaks ill of our savior Christ, he will know through the presence of his alliance. If anyone talks about Jesus Christ and the Bible or anything about Antichrist, he will know. If anyone attempts to go against our savior, he will know. If anyone worships God and reads the Bible and is having church services, he will know.

There won't be any laws, but there will be notifications and logging to see who still has love for Jesus because those who love Jesus and worship God he hates and wants to eradicate them off the face of the Earth, no exceptions. When we started capturing U.F.Os for higher technology, we designed our capabilities to eventually do so in the future. Then, with integrated circuits with their technology, we fell right into their trap. Now with them hanging over our cities, they will have control over every inch of our lives. They will be able to see us and hear us on our cell phones. They will hear us and see us through our cameras.

That's something we aided them in; we set up everything before they got here with the cameras already in place. We did the all the hard work for big brother.

In all this, Christ, this savior, will have had much time to plan by roaming the heavens through the stars to make alliances and plan out every moment so he may be victorious over us for generations to come. You see, the first year with all the healing, love, and all the people being healed from cancer by this beautiful savior—none of that was free.

Everything he did to you will be paid back tenfold, and you will feel the wrath in the future years that he will give for being nice for that two years. Then people started seeing at night smaller ships leaving the big ships flying towards the heavens. Then they started seeing smaller ships flying towards oceans and big bodies of water like great lakes. People started seeing legends fly back and forth and wanted to know what was going over their skies but were afraid to say something.

Now mind you, this savior could talk to extraterrestrials through telepathy through mind control, so our leaders had a major disadvantage and tried to figure out what was happening around us. Plus, this savior had the capability to read our minds to see what we were thinking. So many were careful and trying to figure out what these legions were going back and forth at will in our skies and our waters without regard for humans. As a race of humans, we were outsmarted, and it was checkmate on a chessboard. We had not been harmed yet or traumatized yet, but as the human race, we could sense that we'd been fooled.

This Alliance was resurfacing Atlantis, resurfacing all their old cities. This Alliance was preparing for Mass studying of the human race at a will with no distractions and full motivation. This Alliance was ready to take this time to repair its DNA from the use of human DNA. This Alliance was setting up battle stations to fight the inevitable return of celestial beings, like the mighty Jesus Christ.

During this time, an ice City in Antarctica had risen with great power, ready to fight the Angels who would one day return to claim the Earth. So many had been through much through war, but this was a different war because while you slept, you were watched. And when you talked, you were being listened to. The amazing thing that no one saw was what the Alliance looked like yet. No one notices what they look or sound like—no one but their savior.

Year Three

THE CUTTING OFF OF HEAVEN

This chapter saddens my heart because this will be the first time in history, from heaven down to earth, that there's no longer any connection. This third year will be the reign of the Antichrist. He will, now, be our savior on Earth, no longer with any connection to God, his son, and the Holy Spirit.

This will be the first time in history that man won't be able to look towards the heavens to pray for forgiveness and love from God. We will be officially cut off and unplugged from the heavenly realm. No more asking Jesus Christ to come into your heart and to be born again—the Antichrist won't be your savior; he will now be the one to answer your prayers. He will preach to have sex with as many people as desired; he will preach many riches to all.

No one will be better than the other; all will be equal under his watch. We will all be of the same color and the same creed. There will be an equal distribution from the rich to the poor. No more wars, he will promise. No more anguish, he will promise. Love, peace, and harmony will be under his power and domain. He is the God of Gods and Lord of Lords. You will pray only to him; heaven will now be on Earth, as the Bible has promised.

Meanwhile, God will look down on Earth in dismay because he promised and allowed Satan to reign on Earth for these Seven years.

God's heart will ache because he has done so much to protect humanity over the years in time and space. A place, or school, for God's bride to learn from and be better for him will now be taken over by Evil and damnation.

There will be no prayers coming from Earth. There will be no love coming from Earth. There will be no singing coming from Earth. The sad thing of it all, those on Earth will be so happy for this moment. Man will be able to do what he wants with no preaching of righteousness, no church. Humanity will be allowed to drink, do drugs all day, have sex, and not do any work. You will be free to do whatever you want and be safe and free as long you don't bring up Jesus Christ and the savior. The only savior you will have now will be earthly bound to fulfill all your needs.

This year will be the most amazing year for mankind. Only freedom and love will be preached—no damnation. All the prisoners will be released because there will only be love. Marriages will change; no longer will there be a need to marry under God, only under the Antichrist. There will no longer be transgression between husband and wife. Because we'll all have love, spreading it the way we want, with ultimate freedom on Earth through his regime.

With all this newfound love on Earth, Heaven will be praying for us. Worship and praise will be loud for our salvation in Heaven, filled with countless tears and crying for our salvation. It is then that we will know not what we do, or do not what we see, or what we are in for when the tribulation has not shown its ugly face yet.

Year Four
MAN SEEKING REBELLION

I n the fourth year, men will realize the truth of their new Christ and see the dark side come to fruition. For one, there will be ships over every major city all over the world. In the Bible, this is where it talks about the watchers.

Throughout history, they have watched us and studied our every move and calculation. Keep in mind, we have old paintings in our historical past of flying saucers over us. Now we see why. They watched us. Now with the help of the Antichrist, through watching, the time will be there to control us. Not only that, another problem will have emerged on Earth; pre-existing cities that were once there before the flood will have emerged, like Atlantis and others.

The cities will be off-limits to most humans, and many strange, secretive things will happen on a regular basis. People will start to see giants—like in the old testament—come out of caves and strange creators of unknown origin. People will be afraid to go on simple vacations, worried about their families. To add to that, everyone, young or old, will be made to tattoo this Antichrist's name on their bodies and praise his name daily. Everyone will be made to be chip through integrated circuits to be tracked by the U.F.O. presence above.

This new freedom of no church, no Bible, no preacher preaching redemption and salvation will be glorious at first, but then, it will become frightful. Any child born will be taken and baptized in his name immediately, no exception. If anyone discards his name, he will be subject to prosecution in captivity. They say history repeats itself, Earth will start to look like what man went through in pre-flood.

So, man will start his rebellion, with underground computer systems—the oldest computers he can find. Old TVs will be gathered up, and old radios with vacuum tubes and AC generators to compute information from post to post. Mankind will be able to see a grave mistake in trusting this Antichrist, but it will be too late, and they will not be able to fight back The Alien presence will have control of all of our nuclear capability; they will give us the technology of integrated circuits years ago.

Humanity will have no more universal army, no God to wash them away again. If we take pictures of their ships, they will know about it because everything is run from our cell phones. We have put all this technology in our cell phones now they have become our biggest enemy, preventing the act of taking a simple picture.

So many are trying to communicate off the grid, but everywhere will now be dangerous. People will disappear at an alarming rate in the woods off-grid with giants, monsters, and Bigfoot-like creatures that once stayed hidden. Monster mythology will now come alive to be a threat.

Everywhere we go, we will be watched. Some will go underground to caverns, but communication will be challenging, and even certain caverns will have an alien presence because they came from there, waiting to emerge to this present day. But mankind will have the brave heart of a lion because many remember their teaching that Jesus and God will return to capture the Earth. Will he not stop trying to make better come into actualization? He will rebel to always seek freedom and refuge for his infinite survival. We have been tricked and lied to by a mastermind. All of our most valuable patents will be embedded into a cell phone, and we all have become addicted to it. They will know that.

The power at be will watch our every move to checkmate us. They will be the watchers for a reason. Enoch talked about the watchers; that was our warning, but we could not see. Right now, writing this, we will still not see, being brainwashed and bathing in our vainglory of lavish technology, not realizing a giant cage with a juicy steak inside. Once we enter and the latch falls, there will be no escape.

Rebellion we will seek, using Morse code, underground railroads, and tunneling systems to try to capture some empowerment for the survival of mankind. But we will start to disappear in small numbers. We will pray to God when it seems like there's no answer. When we disappear from the surface, it will make us weaker. We won't worry about spies that can infiltrate and sell us out at any given time. But we will have to keep trying through death and survival of mankind, amen.

Year Five

AGE OF EVE

In the age of Eve, women will only seek glorification for themselves. It will be an age where women will continuously put men down as negative entities that stand in their way of self-glorification. The kids women bear will look at the father not as the head of the household but as one who stands in the way. They will destroy him if he doesn't comply with their wishes.

Women will be cunning and witty, seeking only vainglory for themselves on a constant basis to devour anyone who stands in their way. They will say, constantly, "My kids come first," as if there will be honor behind that and empowerment, not acknowledging that it took two to make those kids and it takes two to raise those kids.

A woman won't care about commitment to marital bonds, only commitment to praise from outside sources like Facebook, Instagram, and TikTok, constantly showing pictures of herself and tattoos of herself with her not-significant-other in the photos. She will be on her mission to feel self-gratitude, build an army to watch and praise her, and have many followers at the cost of risking it all.

At the flick of a wrist, she will be able to have men beckoning to touch and feel her holding much power in her hand for others to seek her love. She will crave lust, trying to pursue her daily feels her soul full of excitement and adventure in her mind. She will not make herself look nice for all, but for many. No man will be able to trust her long because, one mistake, and she will trade him in for another, like a used car. She will be fearless; she will have a machine gun in the closet. She will believe she doesn't need a man because one man doesn't have enough praise to please her.

Men, in turn, will feel the pressure of the family structure that they will no longer have; the control his father, and his father before him, had. When man will roar in the household like a lion, the kids will laugh and keep playing video games and being on the internet because he won't be the lion his dad was.

In his prayers, man will ask, "What have I done wrong? I have shown my family much more love than my father ever gave and his father before him, but I am looked upon as weak."

In the age of Eve, when the Antichrist comes on the scene, women will have their vainglory ready to comply to his wishes; she will have his markings and vainglory all over her body. She will have prepared for lust with a commitment not to one, but many. The family structure will be at its weakest because, at one time, women will be devoted to the one they have chosen to be their mate, and now, that will be lost.

Men will fear taking their mates out because they will be checking followers out on their phones. A woman won't stop to give him attention on a dinner date to see what she will be missing in cyberspace. Men will be frustrated at losing their mate, along with all her attention and love, like when Adam was frustrated when Eve ate and took that first bite, leaving him behind to catch up or else. Their face will read, "I have forsaken you while you were not around. I am not the same woman you fell in love with, and if I want, I can have many lovers through my followers."

Unfortunately, Facebook, TikTok, and dating sites are the modern-day apple on the tree. When the Antichrist returns, the first thing he will do is connect to his social media and our T.V., our cell phones, and our women. He will know Eve loved him and was infatuated with him. She loved his wisdom, and he sang to her and made her laugh while God talked to Adam. Satan was talking to Eve; it was backward. It was supposed to be God talking to Adam. Adam talked to Eve, and

Eve talked to the children. There was one equation in there that wasn't supposed to be Satan.

I want to convey I have nothing against women; it's just the age coming to us for us to go through in mankind. Women have held the family structure together for centuries while men fought stupid wars. Men have destroyed a lot, lacking any common sense. Now it's up to women to get rid of the apple now before it's too late because the things heed a warning and once down this path it only gets worst when Satan returns in the next chapter, Gnashing of Teeth, for the family structure, when Satan returns to obliterate the family structure.

He knows your weakness to be glorified, to be told you're beautiful on a daily basis, to say, "Look at me. I have the best body or nice legs or nice lips," and sing to you like he did Eve the first woman. Put not yourself on Facebook with your husband or kids. It's supposed to be used to find friends, not a fashion show for vainglory. What starts off simple can end up being complex, costing us all to lose family structure in mankind.

Year Six
GNASHING OF TEETH

This chapter is the true beginning of the test of man's integrity. He will lose like the men before Genesis, when God flooded the Earth to regain control. He will lose his ability to rationalize his fate on Earth to survive further; he will seek death, but death won't knock on his door. He will seek refuge in the church, but the doors will be locked. He will bow down to his knees and pray to God, but heaven's ears will cease to listen. He shall shout out to God, "Why have you forsaken us? Were we really that bad?" Once you have a choice with God, you will have no choice with the Antichrist.

With Jesus, you will be able to ask for forgiveness of your sins over and over again. With the Antichrist, the punishment will draw nigh your sin against him. There would be no time for being alone through integrated circuits. All will hear, and punishment shall be at hand. Some will seek to go underground, but there will be no place to hide. The mark of the beast will be everywhere. Even if you go off the grid, satellites will look for heat signatures to capture stray humans who wish to hide against his commands.

This is an exhortation; try to keep all your old electronics that are integrated freely, like the old vacuum tube TV or the radio and amps. Try to keep some of the old phones that your parents used because the Antichrist is the king of integrated circuits. Try to keep old answering machines to relay messages to other loved ones in distress. Before he takes full control, he will seek high and low to destroy the old items like in thrift stores, etc. Because in his era, communication will mean survival, and it will be very limited, because we all have bit the new red apple the age of information has consumed us, which was his plan.

In Gnashing of Teeth, invasion will rattle the core of man's soul inside and out because there will be no privacy to communicate at home. But also ghosts will ravish the home in terror at an all-time high, and heaven will want to come to the rescue.

There was a movie that came out in 1982 called, The Entity. It was based on a true story about a woman in California that was raped and tormented by an invisible entity. Everyone should go back and watch this movie. This is how homes will be ravished and tormented. Men will come home, and their entire homes will have been raped, causing the Gnashing of Teeth.

The sad part is that women will begin to enjoy it because Facebook and other social media have conditioned them to love their entities, giving them this attention. Attention is the modern-day apple that will consume them. When man fails to give them attention, they will now have wandering spirits by the command of the Antichrist to consume them through outside pleasure.

Man will pray for God to help his family, but no help will draw nigh. It's similar in the pre-flood when Angels came down to consume the beautiful woman and take them for their wives. They say history repeats itself; the same spirits will come alive in homes and take man's prized possession in modern times; his wife and children. No weapon shall come against them to stop them.

Year Seven
Preparing For War

As I looked around and took in Heaven, I saw and gaze and witness tender white doves pick up a glorious robe made of gold, filled with magnificent light escape from its corners. God honored the robe by anointing it for His son to go into battle. I also saw a sword emerging from the same light accompanied by a glow of blue radiance, prepared to be anointed.

God spoke about His son and how he has His blessings to bring order to mankind and the Earth which remained to be a place for teaching souls in the physical world.

God rendered to him in prayer saying that His son will be victorious in his quest to restore order where the order has been lost and he shall continue his teaching of the holy life in the land of the living.

We have allowed the beast to roam the heavens to obtain an army through choice, from Galaxy to Galaxy for a thousand years. Who now is preparing his army for war in the land of the living. The beast travels across galaxies for thousands of years so he can persuade others to gather has followers.

John the elder in Revelations looked up from the Earth and witnessed many stars in Heaven being destroyed by Jesus which were the ship's that had chosen the beast's army, going against Jesus. God's son and his army are preparing for a war now. The victory songs will be sung before and after the war is won on Earth.

As the angels prepared for war, the enemy's ships will gear up to fight against God. The enemy will be bigger than some moons These magnificent ships will be heading to Earth now to position themselves position for war. Some would have already arrived in the Kaiser belt and they will remain there and send probes to witness the return of Jesus Christ.

The war will ensue between the non-physical and celestial. When you look at the Earth from the skies like John the elder in Revelation looked from the ground in his vision, you shall find that he couldn't tell that Earth was subdued.

A vision from the sky will show giant ships hovering over every city looking like suns above. Atlantis in which God thrust in the abyssed great flood has risen to claim victory over the Earth. These stars that the elder saw will be battling ship's to claim victory over Jesus and the Angels,to claim to be the Gods of the universe.

The beast will have entities roaming around to possess humans so they can fight on his side. Possession of mankind will be at an all-time high on Earth and he will assume this will go in his favor until he sees the army approaching him.

Jesus will purposely take the scenic route where his army would leave a streak across galaxies, blowing trumpets to declare war which will show who is the Lord of the galaxies and the universe.

The universe will witness many humanoids pick sides in the war,some on God side some on Satan's . In the Bible, one of the ships that got slayed was Wormwood. That poisoned the river's water that the men drank and became sick in Revelations. Those who were not believers in the Messiah will know who God is. Those who are atheist men will change their perception and shall know who God is.

Those who made the pyramids who claim themselves has God's will know who God is. Those who enslaved man on other planets shall know who God is.

Jesus will come through the clouds with a reign of beauty for those to witness who will look up and bow down to their knees and say he is the Messiah. His sword of victory will block lasers and missiles and destroy ships from other worlds. His garment will shine through the smoke and fire in the sky as the battle takes place.

Men who were subdued by the Antichrist will begin to sing from the ground as the war ensues above them. They shall sing Praise Goes To You Lord in every language belonging to mankind . Hands will be raised in praise as the battle ensues.You see all the glorious wings of Angels swarming like bees inflaming the enemy.The Antichrist is whipping out electricity from his hands to war off Jesus and the Angels, the legions of war are insignificant against the almighty Jesus. They are not fighting against man but the one who made man the heavens .

The sun will blacken the moon having 2.5 million aliens in it will be cut out seeing chunks of the Moon floating in space. The sun will also cut out from alien ships in it. Angels swarming like bees of fire in unison raging Havoc on Satan army. You will see the chains of glory be dropped from the Ark Angel to capture this Antichrist, when it touches his body he screams in pain from the anointing of the chains. The scream is so loud it sounds like ten football fields of people at once.

The command of Jesus' voice says "Open now yeah Earth your belly" You see the Earth open her mouth with fire and brimstone. Jesus has the key to heaven and hell, he reaches in his robe of glory and pulls out the key to hell. Jesus unlocks Hell Gates The Antichrist curses and screens saying" I will return" as the glorious chains continually wrap around his body, to capture him and be lowered into the belly of the Earth to no longer torment mankind in the future.

Amen.

www.ingramcontent.com/pod-product-compliance
Lightning Source LLC
Chambersburg PA
CBHW051325120626
46547CB00015B/2406